Robert Louis
STEVENSON

Robert Louis STEVENSON

Poet and Teller of Tales

Bryan Bevan

The Rubicon Press

The Rubicon Press
57 Cornwall Gardens
London SW7 4BE

British Library Cataloguing in Publication Data

Bryan Bevan
Robert Louis Stevenson : Poet and Teller of Tales
I. Title
828.809

ISBN 0-948695-28-5
ISBN 0-948695-29-3 pbk

Designed and typeset by The Rubicon Press

Printed and bound in Great Britain by Biddles Limited of Guildford and King's Lynn

Contents

Illustrations

Acknowledgements

To Dr. Iain G. Brown, Assistant Keeper of the National Library of Scotland for his help and advice.

To David Angus of Bridge of Allan, Scotland for his expert knowledge of Robert Louis Stevenson and his constant help.

To Jean Leslie, a descendant of the Stevenson family for taking me to Swanston Cottage in the Pentlands and North Berwick and much kindness and assistance.

To Galen and Michael Weiser of New York City for their kindness in taking me to Lake Saranac in Upper New York State and to Baker's Cottage with its memories of R.L.S.

To Bill Orton for taking me to the site of the Silverado Squatters near St. Helena in California's Napa Valley, walking and climbing.

To Ellen Shaffer, Curator of the Robert Louis Stevenson Museum (Silverado) at St. Helena for showing me the museum.

To Mike Delahant, Curator of Baker's Cottage, Lake Saranac for his trouble in showing me the R.L.S. museum.

To my sister Winfreda Murray for accompanying me to the Highlands of Scotland and much assistance for a memorable visit.

To Patricia Ellison for taking me to 17 Heriot Row in Edinburgh, the Stevenson family home for many years.

To Lady Dunpark for showing me 17 Heriot Row.

To Andrew Low for much help and driving me on my visits to the Highlands of Scotland and his help in Edinburgh on a further visit.

To Ann Holland for taking me to Barbizon and Fontainebleau and for giving me a book of R.L.S.'s prayers.

To Mr. Upton of the Speculative Society in the Old University Buildings in Edinburgh, who showed me round.

To the Secretary of the Savile Club for his help.

To the London Library for their invaluable help and advice as always.

To Sadika Tancred for her generous hospitality.

To my friends and publishers Anthea Page and Juanita Homan of The Rubicon Press for their faith in me.

Preface

"To travel hopefully is a better thing than to arrive and the true success is to labour," wrote R.L.S. in *El Dorado*. For an author, travel can be a most rewarding experience, especially when he visits the haunts and sites of his subject. For that purpose I visited Edinburgh and the highlands of Scotland, Barbizon and Grez on the edge of the Forest of Fontainebleau in France, and more recently the Napa wine country in California, a district of distinctive, natural beauty. I stayed at Yountville, a small, very pretty township, in the Napa Valley Railway Inn, a curious establishment formerly comprising nine vintage railcars converted into very comfortable suites. The staff were extremely kind and helpful.

California is a country rich in wineries, for there are at least 400 today, while in Stevenson's time there were few during the experimental stages of the development of Californian wine. The oldest vineyard in the valley near Calistoga is Schramsberg, founded in 1862 by Jacob Schram, a German immigrant. Stevenson knew Schram well. While Jacob's stout wife entertained Louis's wife Fanny on the verandah of his house, he enjoyed himself enormously, tasting every variety of Schramsberg Burgundy, Hock and golden Chasselas. Possessing a shrewd business sense, Jacob Schram realized that England would be a splendid export market, for he had a high opinion of English taste. Much of his wine went to London as it still does today. Another much smaller bachelor establishment was McEckron's, run by Louis's fellow Scotsman from Greenock, mentioned in *The Silverado Squatters*, as is Beringer Brothers in St. Helena, "a great wine-house with a huge cellarage in the hills and thousands and thousands of gallons lying ready for the market on maturing". A flourishing winery ever since 1876, for seven years later Beringer Brothers built a sumptuous mansion for the princely sum of 530,000 dollars.

I was eager to visit the site of the cabin of the Silverado Squatters where Louis and Fanny spent their strange honeymoon in the summer (1880). One glorious morning in November when the lovely varied pink, orange and russet colouring of the Californian trees are most radiant, I sallied forth with a kind American friend Mr. A. W. Orton, whose model of the reconstruction of the cabin is now in the Stevenson Silverado Museum at St. Helena. We motored through Rutherford, St. Helena, and Calistoga to the 3,000 acre Robert Louis Stevenson State Park, largely undeveloped, on the shoulder of Mount St. Helena at the northern end of the Napa Valley. The last part of the expedition entailed a lot of rough walking and arduous climbing over loose stones and boulders, a challenge to the spirit of endurance. There is a memorial tablet erected in 1911 by the Club women of Napa, marking the site of the cabin, a disused mine, where he wrote *The Silverado Squatters*. Actually he compiled most of the work in Davos, Switzerland.

If there are rattlesnakes at Silverado today, I do not know, for I did not hear their hiss, but they abounded when Louis was there. His dog Chuchu, "a setter crossed with spaniel", about the size of a sheep, was struck with terror on seeing them.

Curiously enough, Spyglass Hill, mentioned in *Treasure Island*, is reputed to be a portrait of Mount St. Helena. There are no authentic pictures of the cabin except for a drawing by Joe Strong, Stevenson's stepson-in-law, showing Fanny and Louis in one of the second-floor rooms.

The devoted Curator of the Silverado Museum in St. Helena, a town of many Victorian houses, is Ellen Shaffer. Established in 1969, it has many interesting and lovely things, including pictures of Grez, on the edge of the Forest of Fontainebleau, by Fanny Osbourne (Stevenson), 'Monday in Samoa', a picture of a native woman by Joe Strong, a lock of Stevenson's baby hair, aged one year, eleven months, identified by his mother. Her own original portrait when young, hangs there, showing her likeness to her son. Among its treasures are also first editions of R.L.S.'s works. The house today at 608 Bush Street, San Francisco, where he lodged from December 1879 to March 1880 has been rebuilt, but a plaque commemorates his residence there.

What strikes the student of Stevenson in his wanderings most vividly, is the pride and pleasure both France and America take in their intimate association with the great writer. However, it is on the austere, purple moorlands of his native Scotland or in the wind-swept Pentlands that we are closest to the spirit of the man.

Bryan Bevan

I

Early Days in Edinburgh

In the winter I get up at night
And dress by yellow candle-light.
In summer, quite the other way,
I have to go to bed by day.

Thus Robert Louis Stevenson alluded to his childhood in *A Child's Garden of Verses*.

No writer has been more influenced by his infancy and boyhood. He was born in Edinburgh, November 13th 1850 at 8 Howard Place, a street of elegant houses lying north of the Water of Leith in what is known as Edinburgh's New Town. He was barely three, however, when his father and mother moved to another home, 1 Inverleith Terrace. The houses faced north and looked towards the Royal Botanic Gardens. Owing to recent development after the Stevenson's time, 1 Inverleith Terrace was destroyed, making way for 9 Inverleith Row.[1] They were tenants here for four years from 1853-1857, but they considered the house too exposed to the rigours of the Edinburgh climate and thus harmful to the delicate health of their only son. So they found a new home in 1857, a graceful terrace house in 17 Heriot Row, a Georgian house with an Adam chimney-piece, a home much cherished by them, and those who live in it today.[2]

When he was a mere infant, Louis (pronounced Lewis) was nicknamed Smout, and later by his family, Lou. He was the son of Thomas Stevenson and Margaret Isabel Balfour, youngest child of the Reverend Dr. Lewis Balfour, minister at Colinton, a village on the Water of Leith near Edinburgh. Louis was always intensely proud of his forebears, all lighthouse engineers, and family tradition would expect him to follow this career.

Louis's paternal grandfather Robert was a most remarkable and gifted man, whose most important work was the celebrated Bell Rock lighthouse eleven miles distant from Arbroath in Scotland. Sir Walter Scott, who died eighteen years before Louis's birth, records in his diary a visit to the Bell Rock in 1814 and a meeting with Robert Stevenson. However, this lighthouse was only completed four years later. Robert was responsible for the lighthouse system in Scotland, superintending the building of twenty lighthouses round the rocky and precipitous coasts of Scotland, and he was a man of many other engineering achievements. It was a hard life, only suited to a person of great physical energy and good health was essential.

Robert's home was a large house, 1 Baxter Place, with a garden reaching to the slopes of Galton Hill, later much loved by his grandson Louis. Nearby was Leith, Edinburgh's seaport. Thomas, Louis's father, Robert's youngest son, had been born in 1 Baxter Place in 1818.

We know a lot about Thomas Stevenson, owing to Louis's portrait of him in *Memories and Portraits*.[3] As an engineer he had built, together with his elder brother Alan, Skerryvore, "the noblest of all extant deep sea-lights" as Louis called it. He tells us that his father together with his brother David fashioned the Chickens and Dhu Heartach lighthouses. However, Louis considered his finest achievement to have been in optics as applied to lighthouse illumination. In describing his father's character, he spoke of "a blended sternness and softness that was wholly Scottish", yet in congenial company no man could be more humorous and funny. He was both shrewd and childish, a Celt both in sympathy and feeling, "passionately attached, passionately prejudiced, a man of many extremes, many faults of temper..." His emotions were deep, like his son's, but "his inmost thoughts were ever tinged with the Celtic melancholy". It is evident that Thomas Stevenson, extremely religious by temperament, was troubled by too much conscience and prone to take on the sins of the world. His sense of his own unworthiness was carried to such extremes that he might be described as morbid. It was the clash of personalities between father and son, so alike and yet unlike one another, and Louis's inability to accept Christian theology when a young man that caused the bitter quarrels between his father and himself. Thomas Stevenson, in his Victorian obduracy, could never accept that his son, however dear he was to him, could hold other religious views than his own. One curious trait of character is related of his father by Louis, namely his "hot-headed chivalrous sentiment". He actually favoured a marriage law whereby any woman might have a divorce for the ask-

2

ing while no man could obtain one, however much provoked. There appears to have been a curious resemblance between father and son in their chivalrous sentiments. Thomas called himself a strong Tory. He was indeed a strange mixture.

Louis's mother Margaret Balfour was only nineteen in 1848 when she married Thomas. A tall, graceful, animated girl, she was more tolerant than her husband, though utterly devoted to him and very pious in a conventional way. She had a sense of humour and in later life she was very adaptable.

She might be a loving mother to 'Smout' and proud of him, but her husband Tom as she called him, always held first place in her heart. When Louis was barely two years and eight months his mother relates: "Smout's favourite occupation is making a church", "he makes a pulpit with a chair and a stool, reads sitting, and then stands up and sings by turns." One fancies that this occupation was only a temporary distraction, for Lou, like many little boys, liked very much to play with leaden soldiers. At six he was already forming a notion to become an author, to learn to write.

However, he suffered from feverish coughs and chills, which often developed into bronchial illnesses, confining him to bed. Perhaps he had inherited his delicate health from his mother, who was often ill when young.

When he was only eighteen months, there entered the household at 17 Heriot Row, Louis's nurse, a Scotswoman from Fife, Alison Cunningham, the cherished 'Cummy' as Lou called her. She was the formative influence of his early years, absolutely devoted to her 'Master Lou', acting as a second mother to him, and, above all, caring for him in his sick-bed.

Louis's early interest in covenanting history owed much to Cummy, whose religious zest lay in her devotion to the covenanting version of Scottish Presbyterianism. Although she deeply disapproved of novels, playing-cards and the theatre, she possessed a strong sense of drama. Louis would later remember how she fired his imagination, reading passages from the Bible, Bunyan and accounts of persecuted Scottish Covenanters in her rich, dramatic, Scottish voice. He would later tell us the last time he ever saw her. "It's *you* that gave me a passion for the drama, Cummy." "Me, Master Lou," she replied. "I never put foot inside a playhouse in my life." "Ay, woman," exclaimed Louis; "but it was the grand dramatic way ye had of reciting the hymns."

3

Perhaps Cummy's early influence was not entirely beneficial, for his imagination as a little boy was already so vivid he did not need to be continually excited by his nurse. Yet he never forgot what he owed her, dedicating to her later his *A Child's Garden of Verses* (first published 1885).

From her boy

> For the long nights you lay awake
> And watched for my unworthy sake:
> For your most comfortable hand
> That led me through the uneven land:
> For all the story-books you read:
> For all the pains you comforted:
> For all you pitied, all you bore,
> In sad and happy days of yore:
> My second mother, my first wife...

Perhaps Louis later expected a wife to be a second mother to him.

Louis's retentive memory, invaluable for a writer, stored the impressions of those childish days. He recalled 'Cummy' lifting him out of bed, carrying him to the window and showing him one or two illuminated windows on Queen Street "across the dark belt of gardens". They told each other there might be other ill little boys and their nurses waiting like us, for the morning. Sometimes the wretched boy was a victim of delirium, tortured by nightmares so that he would cry out. Then his father would soothe him by feigning imaginary conversations with guards, coachmen or inn-keepers. His obsession with evil and the devil that so markedly characterized several of his best short stories such as *Thrawn Janet* and *Markheim* was not acquired when he was a mature man, but taught him by his strong-willed nurse and conscience-stricken father. His longing for an active life was born in him as a child lying ill, helpless in bed.

He wrote in *A Child's Garden of Verses*:

> Armies and emperors and kings,
> All carrying different kinds of things,
> And marching in so grand a way,
> You never saw the like by day.

So he wrote of "phantom cities" and "phantom armies" until fantasy became part of his nature. The verses in 'The Lamplighter' were a vivid impression of the lamplighter walking up Heriot Row with his lantern and ladder to light the lamp.

For Louis, darkness and evil were ever present in his childish mind, closing him in and inseparable. He tells us:

> Do I not know, how nightly in my bed
> The palpable close darkness shutting round me,
> How my small heart went forth to evil things,
> How all the possibilities of sin
> That were yet present to my innocence
> Bound me too narrowly,
> And how my spirit beat
> The cage of its compulsive purity.

There were happier times. During his boyhood Louis would stand entranced before a toy theatre at the corner of Antigua Street and Union Street on Leith Walk, gazing at scenes from 'Skelt's Juvenile Drama'. He later relates in his essay 'A Penny Plain, Two-pence Coloured', written in 1883 and later published in *Memories and Portraits*, "When, upon any Saturday, we made a party to behold the ships, we passed that corner, and since in those days I loved a ship as a man loves Burgundy or daybreak, this of itself had been enough to hallow it." Long and often he lingered there with empty pockets. The name Skelt always conjured up delicious visions.

Another boyish memory was of his maternal grandfather, Dr. Balfour's manse at Colinton. It lay just north of the Pentland Hills, a country visit in the later nineteenth century, although now an integral part of the city of Edinburgh. Louis describes the Manse in his essay 'The Manse', included in *Memories and Portraits*.

"It was a place in that time like no other: the garden cut into provinces by a great hedge of beech, and overlooked by the church and the terrace of the churchyard, where the tombstones were thick, and after nightfall 'Spunkies' might be seen to dance at least by children." Always the love of nature in his letters and prose, "the birds on every bush and from every corner of the overhanging woods pealing out their notes until the air throbbed with them..."

5

To Louis it seemed a great and roomy house. His memories of his grandfather are of his beautiful face and silver hair, for "none more than children are concerned for beauty and, above all, for beauty in the old"; of the tastes of the old man, his grandson wrote, that he was a great lover of Shakespeare, a skilful embroiderer and especially partial to Port, nuts and porter, "and so do I," added Louis humorously, "but they agreed better with my grandfather, which seems a breach of contract." Louis playing in the gardens at Colinton first learnt to love mills. "Or had I an ancestor a miller?" he quaintly asks.

His much loved 'Auntie', Jane Whyte Balfour, kept house for her father and looked after the multitude of nephews and nieces who swarmed about Colinton. A wit and a beauty in her youth until a riding accident made her blind and extremely deaf, she was one of those selfless people happier to serve others than to reap any reward. Stevenson pays tribute to her in *A Child's Garden of Verses*:

To Auntie

> Chief of our aunts, not only I,
> But all your dozens of nurslings cry.
> What did the other children do?
> And what were childhood, wanting you?

When Lou was seven, he was given a terrier named 'Coolin', a lasting comfort as he lay restlessly in bed suffering from bronchitis. Much later when Louis, now seventeen, was staying at Swanston Cottage, the sheltered white stone cottage in the dells facing the Pentland Hills, taken on lease by his father in May 1867, Coolin was his constant companion on walks. At first the owner and his dog annoyed the shepherd, John Todd, by their thoughtless disturbance of the bleating sheep, but they soon made friends. Coolin was buried in the garden at Swanston, and commemorated by a tablet written in Latin. Here is a translation:

> To Coolin, the gentle and friendly, who in a green old age,
> by some unhappy chance met his death at the place where
> three roads meet, where the hunters are wont to gather.

6

This stone has been set up to his memory by his sorrowing friends. 1869. R.L.S.[4]

Swanston was a lasting inspiration for Stevenson, even when he sojourned in far distant lands. Louis learnt to read when six, and the craving to write came very early to him.

We first hear of Louis's cousin Bob (R.A.M. Stevenson), a boy of ten, spending the winter of 1856 at Inverleith Terrace, Louis's second home. Bob became one of Louis's most intimate friends in adolescence and early manhood. He was the son of Thomas Stevenson's brother Alan, and was always the ringleader in all their childish pranks.

His mother Margaret recorded in her diary in January 1855, when her son was five, that "when made to wear a shawl above his sword, he was in distress for fear it would not look like a soldier and then said, 'Do you think it will look like a night-march, Mama?'"

Margaret Stevenson's diary makes frequent mention of visits to Bridge of Allan near Stirling in the late 1850s, then a booming spa, snuggling in the shade of the Ochils. Louis particularly loved Bridge of Allan, and the place was to influence *Kidnapped, Treasure Island, Jekyll and Hyde* and *The Body Snatcher*, among his writings. There his imagination could brood, and find freedom. The air, too, was healthier than that of Edinburgh for an ailing boy. Margaret wrote on Friday, May 7th 1858, "Smout seems weak to me. Determined to take him to Bridge of Allan. Tom and I go tonight." A day later, "Smout and Cummy come today to the Queen's Hotel."[5]

"Sunday May 9th. Smout had a bad night so we sent for Dr. Paterson." Two days later. "Move to Miss Robertson's lodgings (Kenilworth House)." There you can see a rare Deodar Tree. Despite a bout of bronchitis and frequent colds Lou missed few of his dancing classes. Occasionally the Stevensons visited Perth. Lou's whole family habitually spoke Gaellic.

Louis's first school was Canonmills across the Water of Leith from Inverleith Terrace, but he was unhappy there, and he asked his father to remove him to a boarding-school at Spring Grove, Isleworth in Middlesex. His earliest literary venture seems to have been to dictate to his mother *A History of Moses*, a curious blend of narrative and biblical language. For a time he attended a school in Frederick Street near his home in Heriot Row.[6] When Stevenson attended the Edinburgh Academy School, he was so original and daring that his school-fellows thought him an oddity.

He was at least fortunate during 1862 and 1863 in that he could accompany his parents who were travelling for their health. He visited Salisbury, Stonehenge and the Isle of Wight, and during the summer months made his first visit to Hamburg in Germany. In 1863, Louis aged thirteen, first visited Mentone with his parents. He was to become much more intimate with this resort on the Riviera ten years later. Then a tour through Genoa, Rome, Florence, Venice and Naples, where his mother remembered her son's interest in Pompeii and Venice. Whether this early foreign travel made any particular impression on his mind is doubtful, for Louis never alluded to it.

In boyhood, Stevenson was a voracious reader, delighting in the works of Dumas and his heroes D'Artagnan, Athos and Porthos. Browsing in his father's library he soon became an enthusiastic reader of Walter Scott's novels. Curiously enough he much admired Thackeray's *Book of Snobs*. When very young, his mother would read him *Macbeth*, and he was familiar with almost all Shakespeare's works. Louis learnt to love French literature, for he spoke and wrote the language fluently, and the influence of Montaigne is very marked in his essays. He always read with one main purpose, to become a writer, so he eagerly devoured American authors such as Hawthorne, Thoreau and Whitman. Almost certainly, however, the works that influenced his mind most were those of the Covenanting historians, such as Robert Woodrow's *Sufferings of the Church of Scotland* and James Kirkton's *Secret and True History of the Church of Scotland*.

In 1893 he wrote to James Barrie from Samoa, "My style is from the Covenanting writers. When I was a child, and indeed until I was a man, I constantly read Covenanting books." When he was barely sixteen, Louis wrote a pamphlet, *The Pentland Rising, 1666,* based on his researches in Covenanting history. It was published by an Edinburgh bookseller. The hundred copies sold well because his mother bought most of them. It was inspired by the Rev. Robert Woodrow's work *Sufferings of the Church of Scotland* in which he relates how the prisoners, about 50 in number, were captured at

8

the Battle of Ruthin Green and were brought by the soldiers to Edinburgh. "Bishop Sharp, the President," he wrote, "pushed violently the execution of the prisoners and indeed his blood-thirsty temper at this time made him very odious." Louis's interest in this phase of Scottish history was enhanced by his knowledge that a Balfour ancestor of his mother's had fought at Bothwell Brig in 1679, when the Covenanting rebels had been defeated by Charles II's illegitimate son, the Duke of Monmouth. His imagination, stirred by these events and by his intimate knowledge of the Pentland Hills, brooded on the murder of Sharp, now an Archbishop, on a lonely, desolate moor.

His love of the sea was fostered by his visits, together with his father, on a tour of Scottish lighthouses, for it was Thomas Stevenson's duty to make these journeys as Commissioner of Northern Lights. If these travels were intended to make Louis eager to pursue his training as an engineer, they failed in their object, as he possessed little aptitude for that profession. The arduous journeys by boat, often in appalling weather conditions when a lighthouse engineer would often be drenched to the skin, would have badly affected Louis's frail health, and he could never have stood the rigours of such a life. However, Louis enjoyed these travels in Scotland, preferring Wick in Caithness to Anstruther in Fife, although Wick was bleak enough. Constantly plagued by wind and storm. During the summers of 1869 and 1870 he was inspired by the wildness of the coast between Caithness and the Orkney Islands. As a writer he wished to study the Highland fishermen. "The men," he wrote, "are always drunk, simply and truthfully always. From morning to evening the great villainous-looking fellows are either sleeping off the last debauch or hulking about the cove in the horrors." In 1870 he was on the Isle of Erraid, off Mull, for three weeks, where his father was intent on building the Dubh Artach Rock Lighthouse.[7] Louis's adventures on Erraid, a remote island, were later invaluable in two of his best works, *The Merry Men* and *Kidnapped*. His hero, David Balfour, in *Kidnapped* is stranded there. "A seabred boy would not have stayed a day on Erraid, which is only what they call a tidal islet, and except in the bottom of the neaps (tides), can be entered, and left twice in every twenty-four hours, either dry-shod, or at the most by wading."[8] There, David Balfour, almost starving, "watched for the ebbs to get his shell-fish." Mull was the inspiration for *The Merry Men*, Stevenson's short story.

Louis had a passion for small islands. In September 1870 when he was in Portree on the island of Skye, he embarked on *The Clansman* and had a curious encounter with Edmund Gosse, a writer with whom he was later to form an intimate friendship. Now, as they stood side by side at midnight, a party of emigrants bound for Glasgow en route for America boarded the ship. It was an eerie scene in the light of flickering torches as an inarticulate high-pitched cry rose in the darkness. The two young men - both strangers - remarked to each other how extraordinary this movement of emigrants was. They were fated to meet often in the ensuing years.[9] Louis had a special love for the misty Hebrides. Many years later, as an exile in the South Seas, he recalled nostalgically those days of long ago.

> From the lone Shieling and the misty island
> Mountains divide us and a waste of seas,
> But still the heart is true, the blood is Highland
> And we in dreams behold the Hebrides.

At sixteen Louis was a slender, brown, long-haired boy, with large dark eyes and a brilliant smile. After his first summer at Swanston, Louis became a member of Edinburgh University, but he attended his classes most irregularly and lacked any ambition to shine in the academic world.

Partly to obtain experience as a writer, partly to escape from the ultra-respectable atmosphere of 17 Heriot Row, Louis frequented Edinburgh's underworld after dark, studying, as it were, the bohemians, the seamen and the queer types of humanity he met there. However, friendships made when Louis was eighteen in 1868 with Professor Fleeming Jenkin, appointed to the chair of engineering in Edinburgh University, and his wife were important. It so happened that Mrs. Jenkin was making a return call on Louis's mother when she was introduced to the young man. He impressed her immediately, entranced as she was, by his conversation. Who was this son who talked as Charles Lamb wrote? she asked. This young Heine with a Scottish accent?[10] "I have made the acquaintance of a poet," she told her husband. Both the Jenkins were influential people, deeply involved in Edinburgh's cultural life, and enthusiasts for amateur theatricals. Later on Louis took part in these productions.

In his essay 'Some College Memories'[11] he describes the changes that subsequently befell Edinburgh University. "The chief and far the most lamentable change," he humorously wrote, "is the absence of a certain lean, ugly, idle, unpopular student (himself) whose presence was for me the gist and heart of the whole matter, whose changing humours, fine occasional purposes of good, flinching acceptance of evil, shiverings on wet, east-wind, morning journeys up to class, infinite yawnings during lecture and unquenchable gusto in the delights of truancy, made up the sunshine and shadow of my college life..."

Much more congenial to Stevenson in his early manhood was his admission, as a member, to the celebrated Speculative Society, usually known in academic Edinburgh as 'The Spec'. Its rooms were within the Edinburgh University Old Buildings, a stone's throw from where Darnley, Mary Stuart's second husband, was blown up by gunpowder at Kirk O'Fields. Today above the large fireplace one can see hung the ensign of *The Casco*, Louis's schooner yacht in which he embarked on his first journey to the South Seas.

If Stevenson was a rather idle student in the university, he took a very active part in the debates at 'The Spec', speaking on a variety of subjects. Like Archie Hermiston in *Weir of Hermiston*, Stevenson's magnificent unfinished last novel, he shone in the Speculative Society. On March 1st 1870 he opened a debate on the controversial subject "Is the abolition of capital punishment desirable?" He, himself, favoured its abolition. There, Louis reminds us of Archie Hermiston protesting at the sentencing to death of Duncan Jopp by his father, Lord Hermiston, 'the hanging judge,' a sort of Scottish Judge Jeffreys, wearing "the red robes of Criminal Jurisdiction, his face framed in the whig". Archie cannot rid his mind of the horror of seeing the wretched man hanged. One can imagine Louis at these debates, taking his place by the chimney-piece, the shine of many wax tapers from above illuminating his pale face, the glow of the great red fire throwing his slim figure into relief.

Only a week later, Louis read another paper before the Speculative Society on a favourite subject, "The influence of the Covenanting Persecution on the Scottish mind".

Louis was far more Gallic than Anglo-Saxon in temperament. In his early life at least he always felt a foreigner when travelling in England. For instance, in his essay 'The Foreigner at Home'[12] he writes: "A week or two in such a place as Suffolk leaves the Scotsman gasping ... the first shock of English society is like a cold plunge." With his nervous, restless nature, his gesticulation and his fluent, arresting speech, Louis was more at home in Paris or Fontainebleau than England.

Thomas Stevenson was rightly proud of his only son, encouraging him in his early writings, but he could not conceive that Louis would be attracted to such a precarious profession as writing. Nor could he possibly foresee his later eminence as an author. For some time Louis had been pondering whether he should take up the career of lighthouse engineer. He sensed what a blow it would be to Thomas, and dreaded having to tell him his decision to abandon this career. His heart was in writing, an art difficult to acquire, and he early resolved to become a professional author. Neither his delicate health nor indeed his inclinations suited him for the work of a lighthouse engineer. One day, an opportunity presented itself for Louis's avowal of his intentions during a walk with his father from the New Town of Edinburgh to the village of Cramond on the shore of the Firth of Forth.[13] It took place during April 1871. Thomas, despite his crushing disappointment, said little, deeming it best not to argue or make the boy change his resolve. "Tom wonderfully resigned" confided Margaret to her diary (April 8th, 1871). However, Thomas insisted that Louis should study for the Bar, an extremely respectable profession, and a calling highly regarded in the Victorian circles in which Thomas Stevenson moved. He was well aware that many of his neighbours and friends, despite Louis's undoubted charm, looked askance at his son's strange ways, his Bohemianism, his long brown hair and his defiance of convention. Father and son were a contrast, Thomas with his mutton-chop whiskers, stern and upright, humorous when in the mood, but full of Calvinistic zeal and possessing Celtic defects, and Louis thin, narrow-chested, with bright, brilliant, dark, hypnotic eyes. In the National Library there is a letter [14] to Mrs. Sitwell, a lady soon to enter his life during the summer (1873), referring to a conversation with the Lord Advocate in the presence of his father, who strongly advised him to go to the English Bar. And the Lord Advocate's advice goes a long way in Scotland, added Louis.

For his part Louis abided by his bargain, toiled at his legal studies, though he never had the slightest enthusiasm for the law, and eventually passed his Bar examinations, to be called to the Bar. His father must have known, however, that Louis would be dependent on him financially for several years, for the Bar is also a precarious profession. Louis hardly ever practised.

The experience certainly made Louis more determined than ever to succeed as an author. He worked hard at his writing in Swanston Cottage, and read widely and gradually succeeded in gaining the interest of editors. His legal studies were not in vain, for they influenced two of his later works, *St. Ives* and *Weir of Hermiston*. Occasionally in his later life Stevenson might regret that he could not have combined the life of a lighthouse engineer with that of an author, but it is difficult to think of him other than one, who became a great literary craftsman in his chosen profession by dint of hard work.

II
Louis the Rebel

Oh fine, religious, decent folk,
In virtues flaming gold and scarlet,
I sneer between ten puffs of smoke
Give me the publican and harlot.

In such a way, as a very young man, Louis rebelled against the Victorian values held by the upper middle-class society of Edinburgh to which his mother and father belonged. His hatred of pretence and hypocrisy was certainly influenced by his study of the poetry of Robert Fergusson, Edinburgh's own poet, whom Louis deeply admired. He lived in the eighteenth century, having been born exactly one hundred years before Stevenson's birth in 1850.

Fergusson rebelled against the hypocrisy prevailing in the Edinburgh of the late eighteenth century as Stevenson did a hundred years later. The earlier poet wrote, in his 'Auld Reekie'[1]:

> Why should religion make us sad,
> If good frae virtues to be had.
> Na, rather gleefu' turn your face,
> Forsake hypocrisy, grimace;
> And never have it understood
> You fleg mankind frae being good.

When Stevenson sampled the low life of his native city, he must have thought of Fergusson wending his way to the taverns and of his poem 'The Daft-Day':

> Auld Reekie! Thou 'rt the canty (cheerful) hole
> A bield (shelter) for mony caldrife (spiritless) soul,
> Wha snugly at thine ingle loll
> Baith warm and couth (sociable)
> While round they gar (cause) the bicker roll
>   (drinking cups)
> To weet their mouth.

The Daft-Days in Scotland are the holidays at New Year, Yule, Hogmanay, New Year's Day and Hansel Monday, the first Monday of the New Year. Stevenson likened himself to the dissipated Fergusson, who died at the early age of twenty-four. It may be he even thought he was a reincarnation of Fergusson. In Samoa towards the end of his life, Stevenson was to write to his lifelong friend Charles Baxter alluding to Fergusson as "so clever a boy, so wild, of such a mixed strain, so unfortunate, born in the same town with me, and, as I always felt rather by express intimation than from evidence, so like myself".[2] When Louis was twenty-three, and deeply unhappy because of the estrangement between himself and his parents, owing to religion, he was again to liken himself to Fergusson: "Born in the same city, both sickly, both pestered, one nearly to madness, one to the madhouse with a damnatory breed." Exactly why Louis revolted against the Calvinist and Christian teachings dinned into his ears from childhood is not hard to understand, but it may have been owing to his wide reading rather than the influence of his cousin Bob Stevenson. In his published work Louis constantly stresses the debt Burns owed to Fergusson. Louis certainly seems to have been more successful in his amatory affairs than wretched Fergusson, whose unrequited love for Stella, a married woman and poetess, made him deeply unhappy.

As a student Louis, together with his friend Charles Baxter, annoyed his professors by his inattention. We get a picture of Louis, "slight and insolently supercilious, and Baxter, bulky and insolently solemn"[3] entering the lecture hall, listening for a few minutes, and after exchanging glances of pitying contempt, making their casual exit. However, it is not uncommon, perhaps, for students to play truant. When aged twenty-five, Louis would remind Baxter of the past "when we have been drunk and sober, sat outside of grocers' shops on fine dark nights, and wrangled in the Speculative, and heard mysterious whistling in Waterloo Place and met missionaries from Aberdeen." These days always remained a vivid memory for Stevenson. Writing to Baxter from New Jersey on May 7th, 1888, he says: "It is strange when you think what a couple of heartless drunken young dogs we were, that we should be what we are today."

No writer ever had a more loyal friend than Baxter, and
Louis throughout his life would confide his troubles and difficulties to him. Charles Baxter was almost two years older than Stevenson, having been born during December 1848. He was stocky in
build, and tending to overweight, and very unlike Louis in temperament. However, they sowed their wild oats together in Edinburgh. Later Baxter became a very respected lawyer, known as
writer to the signet, signifying in Scottish law a lawyer, who deals
in business management and civil law as distinct from a barrister,
who handles cases in court. About 250 letters of Stevenson to
Baxter are known to survive, and 50 from Baxter to Stevenson.[4]

Louis had been christened Robert Lewis Balfour (the third
name being for his mother Margaret Isobella Balfour), but he
loathed his third name and told Baxter in a letter from Dunblane
written during the spring (1872) he proposed to take his two first
names in full. "As such," he told him, showing at least considerable confidence in his future immortality as a writer, "will probably be the superscription of my tomb in Westminster Abbey, as
well as the marble tablet to be let on the front of the house of
my birth, No. 8 Howard Place." Stevenson was in fact buried far
from the venerable Abbey in his forty-fourth year.

Louis's bohemianism was no pose, nor a passing phase, for it
remained with him all his brief life, certainly in his travels in
Honolulu and Hawaii and to a much lesser extent even at Vailima.
His eccentric dress, for instance, was much criticized by his father
and mother's friends in 17 Heriot Place. It was the revolt of a
young man against respectability and convention. He wore dark
trousers and a black shirt, with loose collar, and a tie that might
be a strip torn from a cast-away carpet. His jacket was of black
velvet, and it was noticeable that it never seemed good or new.[5]
One must remember that Stevenson was a temperamental boy
emerging into manhood, but there was something unique in his
revolt. It is possible that he occasionally posed.

An amusing story is told of Louis's mother and Auntie driving down the High Street of Edinburgh when they were amazed to
see a strange-looking ragamuffin walking along the pavement with a
bag of bones over his shoulder. "Do look at that queer old-bones-
man," exclaimed his mother. "Oh Louis, Louis!" said Auntie, with

a hint of sorrow in her voice. "What will you do next?"[6] No wonder Louis's parents were very concerned about him.

Much has been written about Louis's sexual affairs with Edinburgh's prostitutes in the city's underworld. They are probably, in part, fictitious, but there is some substance to them. Louis at twenty had strong physical needs, but his adventures smacked of revolt against the convention and respectability of the circle in which he had been reared. It was a period of acute inner conflict, familiar to many young men of Louis's age, and his affairs with prostitutes have received all the more publicity because of the fame he later achieved. Not enough has been said about his ardent desire to study life in the raw, to experience human life in all its aspects. His nocturnal prowlings are reflected in his early poetry:

> I love night in the city
> The lighted streets and the swinging gait of harlots
> I love cool pale morning,
> In the empty bye-streets...

His encounters, too, with all kinds of men and women marked his rebellion against his father's harsh creed. Stevenson, however, was also much influenced by his father in his chivalrous attitude to women of all classes. He opposed the notions, fostered by the Victorian Edinburgh society in which he moved, that these fallen women were outcasts, for he readily romanticized them in his early poetry. Whereas Thomas Stevenson would have favoured rescuing prostitutes from the streets, Louis was prepared to accept them, knowing that some did not regret their way of life and how they earned their living.

Many stories are related about Louis's early affair with a Highland prostitute named Kate Drummond, described by J.A. Steuart in his book as "slim and dark, very trim and neat, with jet-black hair and a complexion that needed no cosmetics to make it rosy and alluring." The stories have the ring of truth, and Louis was indeed attractive to women, with his vivacious conversation and expressive brown eyes. It is related that Kate Drummond gave herself to her young lover from desire and that mercenary, sordid considerations did not apply. It is even said that Stevenson proposed to marry her, and bearing in mind the innate chivalry of his character, it is not impossible, but his father, devout and orthodox, would never have countenanced such a match.

There was nothing peculiar in Louis's enjoyment of the Edinburgh underground, nor his *nostalgie de la boue*, for these sentiments were widely held by the intelligentsia, the young artists and writers in western Europe when Louis was born. Ladies of pleasure abounded in Leith Walk and Rose Walk (between Princes and George Street), parading after dark with a kind of gay, vagrant insouciance. It may well be, that in the sordid haunts which he frequented as a young man, Stevenson was more at ease than in Heriot Row, a breath of freedom for him, as one might gasp for air. There he could study all kinds of men and women, the seaman, thief, prostitute, the vagrant, the chimney-sweep, and shepherd, and with his customary candour and honesty draw them from life. His audience might not understand 'Velvet Jacket' as they nicknamed him, but they respected Louis and did not criticize him. For a writer with his notebook working at his early lyrics, these experiences were invaluable. They would provide him with insight into character when he later wrote essays on fellow poets, such as the fifteenth century French poet François Villon. Louis, however, regretted this portrait, since he could only find artistic evil in him, where others discovered beautiful and human traits. The stern moralist in Stevenson was sometimes at war with the Bohemian. In boyhood he had already been attracted by the dual character of Deacon Brodie (there is a tavern named after him in Edinburgh). By day Brodie followed the respected trade of cabinet-maker, in eighteenth century Edinburgh, but at night he became a desperate housebreaker.

There is no doubt that Bob (Robert Alan Mowbray Stevenson), Louis's first cousin, a brilliant conversationalist and an able art critic, exercised considerable influence over Louis in these early days. When he stayed at 17 Heriot Row, Louis was overjoyed during 1870, saying he felt "at last able to breathe". Together they indulged in all sorts of freakish escapades, such as pawning goods in the fictitious name of John Libbel. Such practical jokes smack too much of undergraduate humour, but Bob was the leading spirit and Louis listened eagerly to his cousin's talk of *la vie de Bohème*.

18

It was owing to Bob's ingenuity that a society was founded known as the L.J.R. (Liberty, Justice and Reverence). Besides the Stevensons, two leading members were Charles Baxter and Walter Ferrier, a professor's son. Louis was deeply attached to Ferrier, described as "a gentle, courteous, patient man, without self-conceit, generous and encouraging towards others and handsome". One of those rare spirits, brimming with promise in the springtime of his life, but destined to failure, owing to his addiction to drink. Later we shall see how much Louis cared for his friend Ferrier.

Another early friend of Stevenson's was Sir Walter Simpson,[7] eldest son of Professor Simpson, the inventor of chloroform. He was a favourite companion when they toured Germany together, studying German in Frankfurt and frequently attending the opera and theatre together. The American artist Will Low described Simpson as "a man with a sincere desire to do something in the world for himself, without apparently any very definite idea as to how he should apply his not inconsiderable talents." He was Louis's companion on *An Inland Voyage*, an early book.

It was a devastating shock to Thomas Stevenson when he discovered the written documents of the Society L.J.R. of which Louis was a prominent member. He was aghast when he read the opening words of the Constitution: "Disregard everything our parents have taught us." It is difficult to imagine in this liberal age how seriously his father - a Victorian - would view his son's conduct. He questioned him closely as to his religious beliefs, and the estrangement between father and son became more acute. Emotional by nature and deeply upset, Louis confided to Charles Baxter in a letter (dated February 2nd, 1873):

My dear Baxter,
The thunderbolt has fallen with a vengeance now. You know the aspect of a house in which somebody is still awaiting burial: the quiet step, the hushed voices and rare conversation, the religious literature that holds a temporary monopoly, the grim, wretched faces: all is here reproduced in this family circle in honour of my (what is it?) atheism or blasphemy. On Friday night after leaving you in the course of conversation my father

19

put me one or two questions as to beliefs, which I candidly answered. I really hate all lying so much now - a new-found honesty that has somehow come out of my late illness ... but if I had forseen the real Hell of everything since I think I should have lied as I have done so often before ... as my father said, "You have rendered my whole life a failure", as my mother said, "This is the heaviest affliction that has ever befallen me." If people only would admit in practice (what they are so ready to assert in theory) that a man has the right to judge for himself, and is culpable if he do not exercise that right, why it would have been better for a number of people - better for Wycliffe[8] and Servetus and even Whitefield (all of them heretics against the established religions of their day) nay and even me.[9]

This is the *cri de coeur* of a young man of twenty-three, desperate to maintain his absolute right to form his own opinions as to religion and other matters. Here was Louis, a mature man, determined to learn to write and to make his living as an author, for during his formative years he had necessarily been economically dependent on his father and living under his roof. He only had a pound a month pocket money of his own. However devoted Louis's father and mother were to him - and Louis certainly loved them - they failed to understand him at this period of his life. In any age, there can be no justification for sons or daughters to reach maturity of thought and character, and to remain in economic dependence under their parents' roof to think their thoughts. So, Louis rebelled and with his hypersensitive nature and over-emotional response, suffered accordingly.

One regrets at this stage that no letters exist from Thomas Stevenson, that honourable man, giving his side of the matter. No doubt Louis was often inconsiderate, staying out late at night, and we know that both his parents disapproved of their son's way of life and of some of his companions. During this prolonged crisis, however, we are aware of Louis's state of mind from his letters to Charles Baxter and his later correspondence with Frances Sitwell, a lady to whom Stevenson was deeply attached.

An interesting work, *The Edifying Letters of the Rutherford Family*[10] is really a fictionalized account of what was going on in the Stevenson family during that crucial year 1873. The fictionalized characters hide the identity of Thomas Stevenson, Louis himself, of his cousin Bob and of Louis's intimate friend in Edinburgh, Charles Baxter. James Rutherford, the father, is Stevenson's father, Paul Somerset travelling abroad is R.L.S.'s cousin Bob, Robert Alan Mowbray Stevenson, while young Rutherford's intimate friend in Edinburgh is Louis's lifelong friend Charles Baxter in his native city. 1873 was a year of crisis for Louis. He confided to his friend Miss Crosby on 7th October,

> My life is a very distressing one at home, so distressing that I have a great difficulty in keeping up a good heart at all or even in keeping my health together. For nearly a year back, I have lived in the most miserable contention with my parents on the subject of religion. ... every now and again I am driven to the most wretched state, to be continually told that you have utterly wrecked the lives of your father and mother, and to see that much of this is true - the wretched truth - is not, you must grant, a very favourable circumstance in cheerful thoughts.[11]

A letter from William Rutherford to Paul Somerset might well be Louis writing one of his intimate letters to Bob:

> As I was saying, I went home in a fine tip-toe transcendental frame of mind, all golden credulity, golden outlooks on the future, and the blue sky of liberty overhead. And when I had deftly turned the passkey, and thought to slip off to bed and trail all these clouds of glory direct into my dreams, what should I find but the house all lit up from top to bottom. "You are late," said my father. "Where have you been?" William Rutherford said he had been at the theatre.

In another letter he tells Paul, "I am full of matter like a champagne bottle and like all persons lying in a state of siege, I have plenty of incidents from day to day to chronicle."

The letters reveal Louis's intense longing to be free of his home environment where he was restricted and misunderstood. In a sense his outburst was designed to champion the rights of other imaginative and aspiring young men in the Edinburgh of the 1870s, not allowed their natural freedom. When he indulged in arguments in the debates of L.J.R. Louis escaped from the tedium of having the ten commandments and their corollaries drummed into his ears to perpetuity.[12] So, the nights of "golden credulity" with his friends where he could be himself. There are indications that Louis was becoming deeply neurotic at this time.

The young Stevenson was absolutely consistent in one matter, his ardent resolve to learn how to become a successful writer. He never wavered from this, despite his troubles at home. He tells us in his essay 'A College Magazine', subsequently published in *Memories and Portraits*, that throughout his boyhood and youth he was regarded as an idler, "yet I was always busy on my own private end, which was to learn to write". He relates that he always kept two books in his pocket, one to read, one to write in. He learnt to love words and might have murmured with Maurice Baring,

> I have loved words that filled my soul with wings,
> Words that are windows to eternal things.

On his walks, as he told Baxter, he would fill the air with dramatic dialogues, taking many parts and writing down conversations from memory. Whenever he read a passage in a book that particularly pleased him, he would sit down and ape that quality. In a much quoted sentence Stevenson admitted,

> I have thus played the sedulous ape to Hazlitt, to Lamb, to Wordsworth, to Sir Thomas Browne, to Defoe, to Hawthorne, to Montaigne, to Baudelaire and to Obermann... That, like it or not, is the way to learn to write; whether I have profitted or not, that is the way.

In his youth Stevenson admired Congreve's exquisite prose rather than his verse and sought to copy it. Some critics have misunderstood Stevenson's tendency "to play the sedulous ape", claiming in a slightly disparaging way that he was no more than a verbal craftsman. To dismiss his books as mere flourishes of bodiless technique is highly mistaken, for Stevenson was not only a troubled moralist, but a writer of striking originality. As David Daiches writes, Stevenson "became a passionate student of topography with a deep feeling for the relationships between place and action". Stevenson reveals more of himself in his essays, his short stories, his fables, his novels and his letters, and in his writings we can know the man.

In one of his essays he describes what he names "fitness in events and places", where a certain locality becomes associated with an appropriate invented action. "Some places speak distinctly, certain dark gardens cry aloud for murder, certain old houses demand to be haunted, certain coasts are set apart for shipwrecks." Thus a harmless old gentleman is clubbed to death on an autumn night in a dark lane in the City of London in *Dr. Jekyll and Mr. Hyde*, a murder witnessed by a maidservant, for her window was brilliantly illuminated by a moon casting its light on the lane. In his letters, particularly to those he loved, we can glimpse how much Stevenson was affected by topography, and in his feeling for nature we can detect the influence of Wordsworth, whose poetry Stevenson deeply admired.

The early scenes in R.L.S.'s life in his beloved Scotland, memories of winter-time when he lived alone at Swanston in the Pentlands, mattered far more to him than foreign travel. They have a lasting influence on his work. In his essay 'A gossip on a novel of Dumas's'[13] he tells us how he would read over and over again *The Vicomte de Bragelonne*, delighting in the antics of d'Artagnan and Athos. He tells us:

> I would return in the early night from one of my patrols with a shepherd (John Todd); a friendly face would meet me in the door, a friendly retriever (Coolin) scurry upstairs to fetch my slippers; and I would sit down with the Vicomte for a long, silent, solitary lamp-light evening.

As he became immersed with the rattle of musketry and the clatter of horse-shoes in the narrative, he would seem to enter another world, and his nights were no longer solitary.

One thing is clear. Stevenson learnt the craft of writing the hard way. Like many creative artists his early efforts were fraught with difficulty and even failure. At twenty-five he wrote his cousin Bob how he struggled to write short stories. To Sidney Colvin to whom Louis owed such a vast debt in his early career, he once wrote:

> I have been working like hell at stories and have up to the present failed. I have never hitherto given enough attention to the buggers speaking - my dialogue is as weak as soda water.

However, new friendships were about to have an enduring influence on his life.

III

His Madonna

Madonna, you are a very sweet thought to me.

It was with infinite relief that during July 1873 Louis received an invitation from one of his Balfour cousins, Maud Babington, the wife of a clergyman, to visit them at the rectory in Cockfield, Suffolk, a small village near Bury St. Edmunds. His parents certainly approved of the visit, and had no objection to Louis going to Suffolk. Cockfield Rectory was a Georgian house, lying in soft, undulating country near the beautiful medieval wool village of Lavenham.

One day in July, a balmy day of an English summer, the slight figure of Louis Stevenson could be seen dressed in a velvet coat, a straw hat, with a knapsack on his back, striding along the road from Bury St. Edmunds. At Cockfield he was given a warm welcome by his hostess, and there, for the first time, he met Frances Sitwell, Anglo-Irish by birth, a beautiful brunette, with small hands and feet, highly accomplished and witty and dainty in her movements.

She was twelve years older than Louis, of some significance for the young man, for he was always attracted to older women. She was a woman of considerable experience, having already widely travelled in Ireland, Germany, Australia, England and India. However, Mrs. Sitwell with some fortitude concealed her own troubles at this time, for she was unhappily married and separated from a man vaguely described as "possessing an unfortunate temperament and uncongenial habits". In that Victorian age it was extremely difficult for an unhappily married wife to rid herself of a husband, however grave the provocation. Bound by Victorian *mores* she could neither divorce her husband, nor have physical relations with another man so long as her husband was alive.

Louis immediately made friends with Bertie, Frances Sitwell's small son, for he had an intuitive understanding of children. Bertie took Louis to see the moat in the Rectory where they could both fish and boat, and Louis made fast friends with his mother Frances Sitwell, a woman of sympathy and intelligence, prepared to listen for hours about his troubles with his parents at 17 Heriot Row.

It was an idyllic month for Louis, those warm days of July, the indolent charm of the garden where he could indulge in long talks with this sympathetic friend, combined with walks in the peaceful countryside, and the pleasure of reading poetry together. It is obvious from his subsequent letters that Louis fell ardently in love with Mrs. Sitwell. On her part, Frances was immediately impressed by Louis, and with insight, detected his genius. She was so fascinated by his brilliant conversation that she wrote to her friend Sidney Colvin, a Cambridge Professor of Fine Arts, critic and essayist, that he must hasten to visit Suffolk to meet Louis. Colvin was five years older than Louis at this time, aged twenty-eight, a man of established reputation. Where Colvin was cautious, reserved and meticulous, Stevenson was highly emotional and passionate by nature. The relations between the two gifted men were all the more interesting since they both loved the same woman. There was a tacit understanding that Colvin would marry Frances Sitwell once she had attained her freedom.

Louis's personality was so striking that few people could resist him, and Colvin wrote of him in those early days with rare insight:

> He struck you as freakish, rare, fantastic, a touch of elfin, and unearthly, a sprite, an Ariel. And imagine that, as you got to know him, this sprite, this visitant from another sphere, turned out to differ from mankind in general not by being less human, but by being a great deal more human than they; richer-blooded, greater-hearted, more human in all senses of the word, for he comprised within himself, and would flash on you in the course of a single afternoon, all the different ages and half the different characters of man, the unfaded freshness of a child, the ardent outlook and adventurous daydreams of a boy, the steadfast courage of man-

hood, the quick sympathetic tenderness of a woman...
He was a fellow of infinite and unrestrained jest and
yet of infinite earnest, the one very often a mask for
the other? a poet, an artist, an adventurer; a man beset
with earthly frailties, and despite his infirm health of
strong appetites and unchecked curiosities, and yet a
profoundly sincere moralist and preacher and son of
the Covenanters after his fashion, deeply conscious of
the war within his members, and deeply bent on acting
up to the best he knew.[1]

It was clearly Louis's personality rather than his literary
achievement, which impressed both Colvin and Frances Sitwell,
for at twenty-three he was unknown in the literary world. To
Colvin, young Louis owed an enormous debt for his belief in him
as a writer and useful introductions to editors and others, who
could help him attain his ambition, and Louis freely acknowledged
his gratitude to his more experienced friend. Frances Sitwell, too,
an important influence, entered his life when he needed her most,
a source of inspiration for a man aware of his genius. Colvin on
his part must have known that Louis was strongly attracted to
Frances, even loved her, but he is reticent about it, and only rarely
resented it. It is obvious that Colvin, knowing Frances Sitwell's
fine character, trusted her absolutely, but Louis's physical needs
were very strong and he almost certainly indulged in wistful hopes
at any rate for some time that this radiant lady would become his
mistress. From Louis's correspondence we can be certain of his
ardent love for Frances, and his hope of a sexual affair with her.
Of her emotions, it is more difficult to speak, because her letters
to Louis were all destroyed,[2] but she was extremely attached to
him. Her position was a peculiarly delicate one, married at least by
law to a man from whom she was separated, with an understanding that she would marry Sidney Colvin when free to do so. She
was too circumspect a character to let her heart rule her head,
whatever her feelings for Louis.

Many of R.L.S.'s letters to her are in the National Library of
Scotland in Edinburgh. It is fascinating to follow the course of his
friendship and to sense his elation at times and the depths of his

despair when on one occasion one of her letters was mislaid.

During the winter months a favourite pastime of Louis's was skating - he was not at all expert. He often went to Duddingstone near Edinburgh. One Monday, he wrote to her,

> Do you know I have been thinking a great deal of you today. When I came home in the snow from Duddingstone at dusk, and again at the concert, Madonna, you are a very sweet thought to me .... It seems so hard we should not be together....[3]

His urgent love for Frances Sitwell made him evermore sensitive to the beauties of nature:

> If you could have seen the moon rising, a perfect sphere of smoky gold, in the dark above the trees and the great hills snow-sprinkled overhead. It was a sight for a King.

Again he writes: "My dear Lady, you are dear to me indeed." He tells her he feels well, "only I have a tendency to get *giddy* at the nape of the neck." Anxious about her own private cares, his Madonna's health was also subject to periodical ailments, and Stevenson worried about her.

On a Wednesday he wrote to her:

> I stayed on Duddingstone today till after nightfall... A gigantic moon rose meanwhile over the trees and the kirk on the promontory among perturbed and vacillating clouds.... I think of you reading it (my letter) in bed behind the little curtain and no Bertie[4] (her son) there and I do think, Madonna, that you love me, and believing that I am not out of hope that I may make this day something more joyful than it would have been without me, which is my best hope in this world, so help me God.

Some time in early June 1874 Stevenson stayed with his new friend Sidney Colvin in his house in Hampstead, and there he saw Frances Sitwell several times. We do not know exactly what happened, but it may well be that Louis had been too ardent and Colvin had resented his manner. Frances was obliged to explain to Louis that she was still theoretically married and that she had no desire to ruin her relationship with Colvin. When Louis returned to Edinburgh, he referred to the incident in a letter, revealing that he felt some touchiness:

> You need not have written to me about S.C. I knew all along there was nothing in it, but my *mauvais coeur* and all I said was that I wasn't to write until the impression had died out and I could write nicely.[5]

Stevenson could never have made a conventional love marriage in a drawing-room of the prosperous middle class. He was very much in love with an older woman. Henceforward, however, he was prepared to write to Mrs. Sitwell as "his mother", for his own mother, however loving she had been in infancy and boyhood, naturally put her husband before her son, especially during the prolonged crisis in their relations. Louis's friendship with Frances Sitwell now entered a more subtle phase. Though he tried to stifle or sublimate his feelings as a potential lover, the yearning for a fuller relationship continued to nag him.

At Christmas in 1874 he bravely writes to her, accepting the position as "her son", though she is still his Madonna:

> Outside it snows thick and steadily. The gardens before our house (17 Heriot Row) are now a wonderful fairy forest and this whiteness of things, how I love it, how it sends the blood about my body. Maurice de Guerin (a French writer) hated snow. What a fool he must have been.... But you will see, dear Madonna, that I am very happy as I write and that will make you happy as you read, will it not? You must be happy. I will not have a sad deity in my chapel, she must be all smiles and peace must look eloquently out of her eyes, and she must not know what doubt is.... So, Madonna, I give you a son's kiss this Christmas morning.... ever your faithful friend and son and finest Robert Louis Stevenson.[6]

The strained relations with his parents continued during the late summer (1873) and on into the autumn. There is evidence on September 9th that Thomas and Margaret Stevenson had transferred all blame from Louis, and had no censure for anybody but Bob. On Wednesday, Louis writes to Mrs. Sitwell:

> I saw Bob at 11.40 p.m. At first I thought he was drunk ... he sank down on a chair and began to sob. The war began with my father accusing Bob of having ruined his house and his son. Bob answered that he didn't know where I had found out that the Christian religion was not true, but that he hadn't told me.... My views according to my father, are a childish imitation of Bob, to cease the moment the *mildew* is removed. All that was said was that I had ceased to care for my father and that my father confessed he was ceasing and had greatly ceased to care for me. Bob had promised never to talk to me about religion any more.

When Louis saw his cousin again he told him that he had received a letter from Thomas Stevenson, apologizing for anything he may have said, but adhering to the substance of the interview. "His father wailed over a ruined life and hopes overthrown, intolerable to think about."

Louis found a whole world of repressed bitterness in his parents' household, with the wailings of his father and his mother having hysterics over it all.

A month later, however, on Monday October 6th, Louis wrote to Frances Sitwell describing a wild moonlight night of autumn. For Stevenson trees with their strange music were always real, possessing souls like human beings.

> The trees are certainly too leafless for much of that wide rustle that we both remember. There is only a sharp angry sibilant hiss like health drawn into the strength of the elements that one hears between the gusts only.

Louis might find consolation in the beauties of nature, but

there was unhappiness at home. "My father is really *mad*," he wrote to Frances.

> I know no other word for it ... this morning he was abusing my mother to me, before the servants.... My mother was very quiet and when she came, paid little or no attention to it all....

He told Mrs. Sitwell that he had finally bid adieu to inheriting any money. "I must live by my pen or something I promised my father." He assured his father that he would never use a farthing of his money unless he was a Christian. His father maintained that he only held his money in trust for the views in which he believed.

> So I said to him that I should reckon any person a thief, who would use another's money in such circumstances and he said fervently "and a damned thief, too". He was quite quiet and sensible, indeed it is the sense of his whole life, and for me it will of course supersede the terms of any will written in ignorance, doubt or misapprehension.

His father suffered from jaundice, but he was soon much better, and the miserable scenes of yesterday did not occur again. "My moral inheritance has quickened me for work again," Louis wrote Frances Sitwell, "but *Ça me fait heureux, il ne manque rien, sinon la présence, ma mere.*" Try as he might to stifle his feelings for her as a lover, Louis never really succeeds in overcoming his yearning for her. He is resigned to his role as "her son", but his demands on her as "his mother" remain high. Perhaps there is something a little neurotic in his love for her.

> Think of me how you must be to me throughout life, the mother's breast to suckle me. If I am to be a son, you must be a mother.

On a Saturday during January 1875 he writes Frances:

I am so happy. I am no longer here in Edinburgh. I have
been all yesterday evening in this forenoon in Italy four
hundred years ago with one Sanazarro, a sculptor,
painter and poet, and one Ippolita, a beautiful Duchess.
O' I like it badly!... What a change this is from collecting
dull notes for John Knox as I have been all the early part
of the week - the difference between life and death....

The letter reveals how much he valued Frances Sitwell's opinion,
for he was avid for her to read it. It was his first little volume of
stories, named when completed, *When the Devil was Well*, in allus-
ion to the old proverb. The story is certainly immature and the
characterization weak, but it has a certain charm.

Sir Sidney Colvin said that the Italian story, so delightfully
begun, was destroyed like all the others of this time.

Sir Graham Balfour, however, Stevenson's first biographer,
assigns the beginning of the tale to the end of 1874.[7] According to
him, it was finished during the following year and the unfavourable
opinion of his friends was accepted as final. One early reader, defy-
ing contemporary opinion, wrote on the last page of the manuscript: "Bravissimo, Caro Mio!" The story was one of his earliest
pieces of fiction.

In Edinburgh, Louis often went to concerts with Charles Baxter. "We have now added Wagner to the list," he told "his Madonna". "He is jolly and fresh, like a wind," he wrote her during
February 1875. A favourite composer was Beethoven, and he delighted in the Eroica Symphony. "Look here, Madonna," he added
to a letter, "when we have the chance we shall hear that symphony
together. Beethoven is certainly the greatest man the world has yet
produced." He told her later about all his activities, including his
part in amateur theatricals as Orsino (the Duke) in *Twelfth Night*
at the Jenkins'. Though he loved the part, he was afflicted with
such a cold in his swollen eye, "So how I shall look as Orsino God
knows..." His mood had changed.

On Sunday the bells were ringing clamorously from
church and as they ring all the weary Sundays of my
childhood go in procession through my heart. O the
ennui, the ennui of it all.

He assured her of his love, but it is hardly convincing as the kind of love a son has for a mother.

His friendship with Colvin had ripened rapidly, but here and there a little tension is evident. He tells her: "I have written to Colvin. I wonder will he show it to you."

His letters to Frances Sitwell certainly give us profound insight into his character, and his defects, too, for instance his egotism and occasionally his self-pity. For two years the friendship was most intense, then it gradually became more subdued, though it lasted for life. She is in his thoughts most of the time, on favourite walks at Bridge of Allan near Stirling Castle, along the riverside among the pines and ash trees and later in France. Louis often stayed there.

The disagreeable scenes at 17 Heriot Row with his father continued. One Wednesday Louis wrote her:

> I tried every wile that I have to thaw him, but he responded in gruff monosyllables. At last he got up to go to bed. I could not let him go in such a mood, so I asked his pardon, and said I was afraid I had spoken hotly. He said I should know there were subjects on which he felt deeply and that I did nothing to save his feelings. Whereupon with the sublime theatricality of the Stevenson family (O we mean it when we do it - don't mistake) I kissed his hand and became ruefully tearful.

He tells her of a curious adventure in Queen's Park trying to protect a poor crazy preacher from a lot of rude boys and brutal old men. His sensitivity makes it difficult for him to bear the misfortunes of others. On September 6th 1873 he tells Frances how he was returning through the wet, crowded, lamp-lit streets singing a German tune when he heard a poor crippled man in the gutter wailing over a Scottish air ... "and the ugly reality of the cripple-man was an intrusion on the beautiful world in which I was walking."

By October Louis was in a state of extreme nervous exhaustion and suffering also from suspected tuberculosis. Telling his mother that he was travelling to Carlisle, probably assuming that

33

she would think he was planning some walking in the Lake District, Louis went to London where Mrs. Sitwell and Sidney Colvin both insisted that Louis consult the eminent specialist in lung disease, Dr. Andrew Clark. It was fortunate for Louis that Clark advised his patient to go abroad and to the south. In jubilation Louis wrote "his dearest friend", "Clark is a trump. He said I must go abroad and that I was better alone." It was with a glorious sense of freedom and with profound relief that Louis prepared for his journey to Mentone in the Riviera, away from the gloom of Edinburgh. His mother had wanted him to accompany her to Torquay, but both parents were now resigned to their son going to Mentone.

Louis always enjoyed travel, especially by sea. He crossed from Dover on November 6th, and travelling via Paris and Sens arrived in Avignon, where he delighted in the walk up the Rocher de Doms. There he read a letter from Frances and wrote to her: "The whole air was filled with sunset and the sound of bells and I wish I could give you the least notion of the southernness of all I saw." He was enjoying the works of the French critic Chateaubriand.

When he first arrived in Mentone, Louis was near a nervous breakdown, and felt very depressed. Charles Baxter wrote to him on November 16th in an insular way asking whether the sky was blue.

> Is the song of the labourer heard in the morning and do you hate existence no more? Is it better to be a Mentonian (I'm blessed if I know where the place is) than a Scotchman? Are his wives prettier?

Stevenson soon became very attached to Mentone, but he was unhappy at first. However, under the spell of this beautiful place with its sunshine and lemon and orange trees, Louis gradually regained his health.

It was in Mentone that Louis composed his important essay 'Ordered South', which was eventually published in *Macmillan's Magazine* and can now be read in *Virginibus Puerisque*.[8] It is written in a curiously detached, almost impersonal way, but is highly original, as most of his writings are. He wrote: "Nothing can change the eternal magnificence of form of the naked Alps behind Mentone." Perhaps he had been to Ste-Agnes, that beautiful village in the hills. "Nothing, not even the crude curves of the railway, can utterly deform the suavity of contour of one bay after another the whole reach of the Riviera." And of all this, he has only a cold head - knowledge that is divorced from enjoyment. He recognizes with his intelligence that this thing and that thing is beautiful while in his heart of hearts he has to confess that it is not beautiful for him."

So, while this mood prevailed, Louis wrote to Frances Sitwell:[9]

> Being sent to the South is not much good unless you take your soul with you, you see. Go South! Why I saw more beauty with my eyes healthfully alert to see in two wet, windy February afternoons in Scotland, than I can see in my beautiful olive gardens and grey hills in a whole week in my low and last estate.

He occasionally calls his Madonna, *Consuelo de mi Alma*, in letters from Mentone.

Then the artist in him responding to the joy of seeing the first violet. He wrote Frances:

> There is more sweet trouble from the heart in the breath of this small flower, than in all the wines of all the vineyards of Europe.... I feel as if my heart were a little bunch of violets in my bosom, and my brain is pleasantly intoxicated with the wonderful odours. No one need tell me that the phrase is exaggerated if I say that a violet *sings*. It sings with the same voice as the March blackbird, and the same adorable tremor goes through one's soul at the hearing of it.[10]

Stevenson spent the first month in the Hôtel du Pavillon, but he felt humiliated because his father was paying for his stay in Mentone. Louis would remain dependent on his father for some years, though he made various attempts to gain his freedom.

35

Louis admitted to Frances Sitwell that he sometimes took opium, used medicinally as a painkiller and sedative. One Monday he tells her:

> I had been rather seedy during the night and took a dose in the morning and first time in my life it took effect upon me. A day of extraordinary happiness and when I went to bed there was almost something terrifying in the pleasures that besieged me in the darkness. Wonderful tremors filled me. My head swam in the most delirious but enjoyable manner, and the bed softly oscillated, like a boat in a very gentle ripple.

When Sidney Colvin visited Louis in Mentone towards the end of December, they moved from the Hôtel du Pavillon to the Hôtel Mirabeau, renowned for its excellent food. There Louis indulged in a harmless flirtation with two Russian ladies, Mme Zassetsky and Mme Garchine - both sisters, but he took as much pleasure in the society of their children, especially in a three-year-old, who kept him much amused. For their part, the Russian ladies were evidently much attracted by Louis, and may have wanted an affair with him. Louis and Colvin enjoyed themselves enormously in Monaco. "We have been out all day in a boat," Louis wrote to Mrs. Sitwell,

> Lovely weather and almost dead calm. Our boatman was a man of delightful humour, who told us many tales of the sea, notably one of a doctor, who was an English man and who seemed almost an epitome of vices, drunken and dishonest and utterly bad.[11]

Colvin was already devoted to Stevenson, but he was not as an amusing companion as Bob or Baxter. He could not enjoy any adventure without saying that he regretted Frances Sitwell was not there, "and I have not quite enough countenance to make any answer." They had a very social time, dining with Sir Charles and Lady Dilke. "I liked the Republican," added Louis.

Stevenson was far from idle in Mentone, for in January he

was working on an essay on Walt Whitman.[12] Fascinated by Whitman's poetry, his studies of him may well have fostered an ardent desire to visit America. Here Stevenson tries to steer a middle course between "an excess of unadulterated praise" and a fastidious public, blind to an inspiring writer. He was also planning a book to be named *Four Great Scotsmen*, John Knox, David Hume, Robert Burns and Walter Scott, but in reality he eventually wrote only two essays on Burns and Knox. He was reading much Scottish history, storing in his capacious mind impressions to be used much later when he came to write *Kidnapped, Catriona, The Master of Ballantrae* and *Weir of Hermiston*.

While Louis and Colvin were in the south of France, the poet and essayist Andrew Lang called on Colvin. Thus was Lang's first acquaintance with Stevenson, but Lang, a fellow Scot, was at first unfavourably impressed by Louis's smooth face and long hair. He did not approve of his wide blue cloak, which he criticized as un-English and certainly not Scottish. When Colvin was in Paris he had been commissioned by Stevenson to buy him a cloak "piratical in appearance" and dark blue in colour.

However, Andrew Lang's acquaintance with his fellow Scot was to ripen into a fast friendship. He was six years older than Louis, and they were later fellow members of the Savile Club, but he never approved of Louis's eccentric dress. Many years later walking along Bond Street, Lang encountered Louis dressed in a black shirt, red tie, black brigand coat, and velvet smoking cap. He was horrified.

> No, no, go away, Louis, go away. My character will stand a great deal, but it won't stand being seen talking to a "thing" like you in Bond Street.[13]

Lang, however, was wont to suggest ideas for books to Louis, proposing some years later that he should write the story of Prince Charles Edward (Bonny Prince Charlie). Although Louis was attracted to the subject, the venture came to nothing.

After five months in Mentone, and feeling restored in health, Louis moved on to Paris, where he had the stimulating company of his artist cousin Bob. Bob introduced him to the *Quartier Latin*, and to various struggling artists and writers living there. As a beginner in the art of writing, Louis was dazzled by Victor Hugo's novels, *Nôtre Dame de Paris*, and especially by *Les Misérables*, and in this congenial environment he managed to work on much of his essay on 'Victor Hugo's Romances', later to be published by Leslie Stephen, the eminent editor of *The Cornhill* in August 1874. Such was Louis's admiration for this great writer - and he was often a moralist in his essays - he can find hardly any blemishes in *Les Misérables,* praising him for his literary restraint.[14] What interested Stevenson was Hugo's moral intention to awaken his readers "to the great cost of this society that we enjoy and profit by, to the labour and sweat of those who support the *litter*, civilization, in which we ourselves are so smoothly carried". In introducing Stephen to Stevenson, Colvin did his friend an inestimable service for which Stevenson was very grateful. However, he soon became aware that it was hardly possible to make a living from essay-writing.

Once he returned to Edinburgh his relations with his father Thomas Stevenson became more relaxed, and definitely improved. Without his father's financial help, an arrangement whereby he gave his son £84 per annum, an allowance to cover all his personal expenses, Louis would surely not have survived. Unfortunately it was paid to him in monthly instalments of seven pounds, and Louis, careless with regard to money and generous by nature to his friends, never learnt to handle his finances, thus frequently getting into debt.

He continued to write to Frances Sitwell, letters expressing his sensitivity, and sense of wonder. One Thursday he wrote to her:

> It is a fine strong day, full of wind. The trees are all crying out in the darkness; funny to think of the birds asleep outside on the tossing branches; the little bright eyes closed.... the little hearts that beat so hard and thick (so much harder and thicker than ever a human heart) all still and quieted in deep slumber in the midst of this noise and turmoil.

He would tell her of his walks in the Pentlands - a matter of three miles - to Glencorse to a church (now a ruined chapel) where Mr.

Torrance, aged over eighty, preached his sermons. Many years later in *Weir of Hermiston*, written in the South Seas, the sights and sounds of those memorable days in Scotland would return to him, particularly of the church where Archie first sees the younger Kirstie, the girl he falls in love with. Below the hills and rough lane where the church stands is a burn and Stevenson must have often listened to its gentle murmur.

There was the sound of bugles as Louis walked one night along Princes Street. "There is something of unspeakable appeal in the cadence," he wrote Mrs. Sitwell.

> I felt as if there must be warm hearts and bright fires waiting for one up there, where the buglers stood on the damp pavement and sounded their friendly invitation forth into the night and I was feeling at the time so lonely and sad.

Although Stevenson wrote among his early books *Edinburgh Picturesque Notes*,[15] he both loved and even occasionally hated his native city, however familiar he was with Edinburgh. He detested its climate, for instance, knowing it was inimical to him, and he had experienced unhappiness there, as well as joy.

By 1874 Louis had a growing sense of confidence that he had embarked on his chosen profession, and despite occasional depression he was achieving something.

IV

Literary Friends

One of Stevenson's earliest works, a story called *An Old Song*, is very little known. It is a work of fiction, very immature in its treatment, and the main female character, Mary Rolland, never comes alive. The scene is Scotland in the not distant past, and concerns the rivalry between two cousins, one of whom returns ultimately to destroy the other. Although Stevenson possessed, like Chaucer, much cheerful faith in human nature, he was as a young man very aware of the evil in men and women. This profound sense of evil was not acquired in his later more polished works such as *Dr. Jekyll and Mr. Hyde* (1885), *The Master of Ballantrae* (1887) and *The Ebb-Tide* (1891). *The Master of Ballantrae*, a widely acclaimed novel, though it has flaws, is about two brothers bent on destroying one another. Stevenson's sense of the possibility of good and evil combined in others, is there from the beginning, and his own character may be described as dual, the moralist influenced by his early beliefs conflicting with the Bohemian.

During the summer of 1874, a year when Louis made important new literary friendships, he was in London staying with Sidney Colvin in his Hampstead cottage. Colvin, always generous in launching Louis's career, proposed him for the exclusive Savile Club, then in Savile Row, a club that had only been founded five years before. There, Louis was eagerly sought for his fascinating talk, and there he would meet the editor of *The Academy*, to whom the aspiring writer later contributed various articles. There, too, ripened the friendship between Stevenson and Edmund Gosse, then a young poet and critic working at the Board of Trade,[1] for they would lunch together four or five times a week when Louis was in London. Famous people, like the Prince of Wales (later Edward VII) and Mr. Gladstone, might occasionally be seen in the precincts, but it was the talented young literary men who held sway in the Savile.

Leslie Stephen, one of those kindly editors always ready to assist talented writers, on one occasion asked both Stevenson and Gosse to dinner. Gosse recollects Stephen's long, thin, bright red beard radiating in a fan shape. During the meal a female novelist, the only guest other than themselves, seemed to be indulging in "a sort of dialogue with itself", and Stevenson and Gosse had the greatest difficulty in refraining from succumbing to a helpless fit of giggling.

When Louis saw his Madonna in London this summer he behaved in too ardent a manner, and she rebuffed him, again explaining the delicacy of her position. Thoroughly ashamed, he wrote to reassure her that she was to remain "as *the sun* that is to shine on all, do good to all, encourage and support all."

When Leslie Stephen was in Edinburgh during February 1875 to lecture on mountaineering, he did Louis a good turn by taking him to visit W.E. Henley, the poet and critic, who was in the infirmary, suffering from a tubercular disease. He was a cripple, having already had a foot amputated. Louis told his Madonna

> that Leslie Stephen called on me and took me up to see a poor fellow, a bit of a poet, who writes for him, and who has been eighteen months in an infirmary. It was very sad to see him there, in a little room with two beds and a couple of sick children in the other bed ... the poor fellow sat up in his bed with his hair and beard all tangled and talked as cheerfully as if he had been in a king's palace. He has taught himself two languages since he has been lying there. I shall try to be of use to him.[2]

Henley was boisterous and piratical by temperament, a large, broad-shouldered man with a copious reddish beard. A fine critic of literature, and poet, he is little read today, though his tremendous courage against adversity and poor health can be perceived in his famous poem *Invicta*. Here is the third verse:

It matters not how strait the gate
How charged with punishments the scroll
I am the master of my fate
I am the captain of my soul.

Both Stevenson and William Ernest Henley had this bond -
they suffered from wretched health. He was the son[3] of a Glou-
cester bookseller, and their meeting in the infirmary was to develop into an important friendship.

Later Louis wrote his Madonna:

Henley's sonnets *In Hospital* taken for *The Cornhill*,
he is out of hospital now and dressed, but still not too
much to brag of in health, poor fellow.

He told her that he was playing Orsino every day in all the pomp
of Solomon and that his clothes were heavy with gold and stage
jewelry. "I play it ill enough," he added.

Stevenson and Henley were intimate friends for some years,
though later estranged. Henley described his new friend,

Bold-lipped, rich-tinted, mutable as the sea,
The brown eyes radiant with vivacity.
There shines a brilliant and romantic grace,
A spirit intense and rare, with trace on trace
Of Passion, impudence and energy.
Valiant in velvet, light in ragged luck,
Most vain, most generous, sternly critical
Buffoon and poet, lover and sensualist,
A deal of Ariel, just a streak of Puck,
Much Antony, of Hamlet most of all,
And something of the shorter-Catechist.

His pet name for Louis was "Lewkin". Louis was very kind to
Henley during his convalescence, taking him for drives in the spring sunshine to see the resplendent cherry-blossom. "The look on
his face was a wine to me," Louis wrote to Frances Sitwell.

During the spring of 1876, Louis "in capital health" was
working hard on several ventures, rewriting a story intended for

Blackwoods, and trying Leslie Stephen to see whether he would be interested in an article about the Raeburn Gallery in Edinburgh. He was working quietly at Swanston, and reading a lot of fifteenth century French history about Joan of Arc, Paston Letters, also Boswell by way of a bible."I have a thing in proof for *The Cornhill* called *Virginibus Puerisque*," he proudly wrote Mrs. Sitwell. These essays he later dedicated to William Ernest Henley, writing to him from Davos in Switzerland in 1881. He was also writing his witty essay in his own original style named 'A defence of Idlers' (which is really a defence of R.L.S.) Louis told Frances. It was later published in *Virginibus Puerisque*, light and entertaining, but full of insight and wisdom. His letters are always characteristic of him, never tedious or priggish. "If you were to ask a squirrel in a mechanical age for his autobiography," he wrote in the same letter, "it would not be very gay. You see I compare myself to a lighthearted animal." And Louis with his brown, flashing eyes, was he so unlike a brown squirrel, a rare species fast disappearing from our land?

About this time Stevenson also wrote a highly original and well researched essay entitled, 'John Knox and his Relations to Women', to be published during September 1875 in *Macmillan's magazine*. It was later reprinted in *Familiar Studies of Men and Books*. Knox was notorious for his book *The First Blast of the Trumpet against the Monstrous Regiment of Women,* which seems strangely outdated today when women take such a prominent part in every walk of life. Knox indeed lived during the sixteenth century in an age when women such as Elizabeth I and Marguerite of Navarre played a conspicuous part upon the stage of European history, but Elizabeth's half-sister Mary Tudor was responsible for banishing John Knox from England to Geneva (1556-1559) where he lived as minister of a church. Strained, too, were his relations with Mary Stuart (Queen of Scots) with whom he had three interviews, but Knox deftly evades the question when Mary confronts him, asking, "You think, then, that I have no just authority?" And whatever Knox's sentiments were regarding a woman's ability to rule, his own relations with his two wives were far from inharmonious and in his later life he had many women friends.

So, Louis passed the early months of 1875, visiting Colvin in Cambridge, frequently resorting to the Savile Club in London, and going on walking tours in Scotland.

Among Louis's intimate friends was Will Low, the American artist. He first met Low when he was visiting in the spring of 1875 his cousin Bob in Paris. When Louis arrived at the St. Lazare Station, Low was at once impressed by the Scot's enormous charm. Low wrote in his book *Chronicle of Friendships*:[4]

> I had heard much of this cousin, of the life which Bob and he had led in Edinburgh where the revolt against the overstrict conventionality of that famous town had been flavoured with the zest of forbidden fruit. I had heard in detail of escapades, innocent enough, the outcome of boyish spirits, in which both had shared, and of which Bob philosophically enough, had borne the blame of leading the younger cousin into mischief.

According to Low, Bob was much the more dominant of the two cousins at this period. He gives one of the best descriptions of Louis:

> He was unspeakably slight, the eyes widely spaced, a nose slightly aquiline and delicately modelled, the high cheek bones of the Scot, a face which in repose was not, I fancy, unlike that of many of his former comrades in his native town. It was not a handsome face until he spoke, and then I can hardly imagine that any could deny the appeal of the vivacious eyes, the humour and pathos of the mobile mouth, with its lurking suggestion of the great god Pan at times, or fail to realize that here was one so evidently touched with genius that the higher beauty of the soul was his...[5]

He tells us that Stevenson's hair never was black, though as he grew older it became a darker brown of the deepest hue. When they first met and for some years afterwards "it was very light, almost of the sandy tint we are apt to associate with his countrymen."

44

Springtime in Paris! How joyful and full of confidence the young men must have been! Their spirits soared as they walked the streets, the sunlight softly dappling the buildings. Louis in his velvet jacket and his companions would walk to a bench on the Pont des Arts on the Seine which looked onto the Louvre, talking furiously about life and art until it was time to eat at their favourite restaurant, Lavenue's.

Low was very fond of Bob Stevenson, and he was to get to know Louis very well, later on, in the artists' colonies at Barbizon and in the delightful villages in the neighbourhood of the forest of Fontainebleau. Paris and Fontainebleau were both important for Stevenson, and these early memories of that beautiful city were to give him useful material for *The Wrecker*, one of his later works.

During June while Louis was at Heriot Row, there stayed at his parents' home a former official of the Customs and Marine Department of New Zealand. Louis was entranced when the official spoke enthusiastically about the beauty of the South Sea Islands. "Till I was sick with desire," wrote Louis to Frances Sitwell. The idea lingered in Louis's memory and may well have influenced his later decision to travel to the South Seas.

It gave Louis a great deal of satisfaction to pass his law examinations and to be admitted to the Scottish Bar in July, 1875, but he never seriously intended to practise. All the same, he was proud of the brass plate reading R.L. STEVENSON ADVOCATE erected on the door of 17 Heriot Row, and there is a portrait of him in his barrister's robes, wearing his wig.

About this time Stevenson was working on an article about Robert Burns for *The Encyclopedia Britannica*, but it was rejected as being "too frankly critical, and too little in accordance with Scotch tradition". Later it was given the title 'Some Aspects of Robert Burns' and published in *The Cornhill Magazine* (October 1879) and reprinted in *Familiar Studies of Men and Books*.

It is possible to view Stevenson as too stern a moralist in this essay, and he may well have been influenced by his Covenanting background, but for a writer the truth is the most important criteria. Was Burns really "a proud, headstrong, impetuous lad, greedy of pleasure, greedy of notice"; in his own phrase "panting after distinction"? Stevenson begins his essay:

To write with authority about another man, we must have fellow-feeling and some common ground of experience with our subject. We may praise or blame according as we find him related to us by the best or worst in ourselves; but it is only in virtue of some relationship that we can be his judges, even to condemn.

One cannot quarrel with his aim.

Both Burns and Stevenson were Bohemians at heart, having a penchant for *nostalgie de la boue*, and both were Scots by birth. One might expect Stevenson to have more sympathy for Burns as an alleged seducer of women. He writes:

> He sank more and more towards the professional Don Juan. With a leer of what the French call fatuity he bids the belles of Mauchline beware of his seductions; and the same cheap self-satisfaction finds a yet uglier vent when he plumes himself on the scandal at the birth of his first bastard.

There was a taint of vanity also in Stevenson's character, and he may well have boasted of his conquests in Edinburgh's underworld. However brilliant the essay may appear to us, it was natural for his fellow Scots to protest at the substance of the essay, for it ill-fitted with the traditional portrait of their national poet.

Thomas Stevenson generously gave his son £1,000 when he was admitted to the Scottish Bar, but he knew Louis's heart was in his writing and that he had no real intention of practising in the legal profession. Louis subsequently squandered much of the money.

Louis's book *An Inland Voyage* was an account of a canoe journey with his friend Sir Walter Simpson from Antwerp to Pontoise. It is lively and entertaining, but rather uneventful. One experience, however, gives it some individuality when Louis, no doubt dressed in ragged clothes, was arrested as a vagrant by the gendarmerie at Chatillon-sur-Loire. The book was eventually published in 1878. Low described Walter Simpson:

46

His was a slow-fighting mind ... shy of his virtues and his talents ... he had an honest stubbornness in thinking, and would neither let himself be beat nor cry victory.

He was a man with

a sincere desire to do something in the world for himself, without apparently any very definite idea as to how he should apply his not inconsiderable talents.

The bitter cold of an Edinburgh winter (1875-1876) made Louis long for warmer climes. It was during the summer of 1876 that he was to visit Grez-sur-Loing, situated on the border of the forest of Fontainebleau and there unexpectedly to meet the lady he was eventually to marry.

V

Barbizon and Grez

Fanny Vandegrift, Louis's future wife, was an American of Dutch-Swedish origin, eldest daughter of Jacob Vandegrift from Philadelphia, who had moved to Indianapolis and prospered in the lumber business.[1] Her mother was a tiny, pretty woman named Esther Keen, who had married Jacob in Philadelphia in 1837. Fanny's father was handsome, deep-chested, his most notable feature being a pair of penetrating blue eyes. Fanny's eyes, however, were black. Born on March 10th 1840, as a little girl, Fanny was extremely pretty with a clear olive skin and masses of dark hair. She was a tomboy roaming the woods, climbing trees and was very adventurous which proved a useful preparation for her future travels with Louis Stevenson. When she was seventeen, she was first married to Samuel Osbourne during December 1857, a gay and attractive Kentuckian. Their daughter Isobel (Belle) was born the following year.

When Civil War between North and South overwhelmed America, the Osbournes declared for the North, and Samuel served for a time as a captain in the army. Later he was employed as a Clerk of the Justices Court in Virginia City, but he never settled in any profession. Instead, he hoped to make a fortune by striking gold in Montana. Her marriage was happy for some years, but he was unfaithful to her and she naturally resented it. For several years they lived in San Francisco where Fanny gave birth to a son Lloyd, named after a good friend, a lawyer John Lloyd. However, Fanny was not prepared to tolerate her husband's infidelity and returned to her parents' home in Indiana. There was later a temporary reconciliation when she gave birth to a second son Hervey, a cherubic infant born in a cottage full of roses in Oakland near San Francisco.

48

By 1875 it was clear to Fanny that her marriage was breaking up. She contemplated the possibility of obtaining a divorce, but it was difficult in those days and because of her family of three she was loathe to pursue it. She took up studying art with her daughter, and with the intention of pursuing her studies, she took her children to Europe. After travelling to Antwerp during November 1875, a difficult place to study art, they moved on to Paris where they worked hard at their drawings, taught by Monsieur Tony Fleury.[2]

It was there that a great sorrow befell Fanny. Her younger son Hervey succumbed to a disease "Scrofulous tuberculosis".[3] The anguish Fanny suffered on account of the death of Hervey, a lovely golden-haired little boy, would haunt her many years later in the South Seas.

Grief-stricken, listless and very poor, Fanny and Belle remained on in Paris until an acquaintance, an American sculptor named Pardessus whom they had met at the Art School, told them about Grez, a very pretty village on the edge of the Forest of Fontainebleau, "a cluster of houses, with an old bridge, an old castle in ruin, and a quaint old church". Thus it was that Stevenson described Grez in *Forest Notes*. Accompanied by Sam, who had joined his family before Hervey's death, they made for Grez. There was to be no reconciliation and Fanny's husband soon departed for America. It was a fateful decision for Fanny and her daughter, for Grez was then a haunt for cosmopolitan, male artists where women were rather looked at askance. Fanny, Belle and Lloyd, stayed at the old Pension Chevillon, "the inn garden descending in terraces to the river".

Will Low, Louis's American friend, writes of Fanny Osbourne:

> One evening at Grez we saw two new faces, mother and daughter, though in appearance more like sisters, the elder slight with delicately moulded features and vivid eyes gleaming from under a mass of dark hair, the younger of more robust type in the first bloom of womanhood.[4]

Fanny was thirty-six, while Belle was a seductive seventeen. It is probable but by no means certain that Louis first met Fanny during the early summer at Grez, even today a beautiful, unspoilt village.

But it was Will Low who first introduced Louis to Siron's Inn[5] at Barbizon, in 1876, a small village not far from Grez, inhabited by Bohemian artists on the border of Fontainebleau Forest. He became very intimate with the district owing to his liking for long walks and canoeing on the river. A Bohemian by temperament, he felt very much at home with the artists who frequented it. Low describes Siron's Inn,

> built round a court, a rambling structure giving evidence of gradual growth and added construction as necessity had arisen. The dining-room looked on the village street and was panelled with wood, on which all my and the previous generation had painted rather indifferent sketches. Long tables ran round three sides of this room, a piano which was inured to hard usage was in one corner and a fireplace in the other. For five francs a day for food and lodging the artists could fare very well. One can imagine the scene as M. Siron cries, "a table, Messieurs!" bearing through the court the first tureen of soup.

Louis knew the forest not only during the day, but "the woods by night in all their uncanny effect". "These trees," as he describes them, "that go streaming up like monstrous sea-weeds and waver in the moving winds like the weeds in submarine currents." The juniper trees form the natural vegetation of the forest, but the Scotch pines reminded him of his beloved Scotland. One of his favourite parts was the Gorge de Franchard with its *ermitage*, once a haunt of hermits, and immortalized in his short story *The Treasure of Franchard*. "Near the Gorge d'Apremont," he wrote, "you find a walk of sand and boulders and of rocks."

In September later that summer Louis, sailing in his canoe, reached Grez at dusk. Bounding through the window of the Pension Chevillon, where a little group of artists were seated at the long table, he was greeted by cheers and exclamations of delight. Among eighteen men at the table were Fanny and Belle, and Louis on being introduced to Fanny, afterwards declared that it was love at first sight according to Nellie Sanchez, his future sister-in-law. He always liked older women. Frances Sitwell was eleven years older than Louis when he first met her in Suffolk, while Fanny Osbourne was at least ten years older during those halcyon days at Grez. Another curious coincidence was that both women had children. Louis loved children, though he was never to have offspring of his own.

It is hardly necessary to relate that Louis's inseparable cousin Bob was with him at Grez. Lloyd Osbourne, then a short-sighted school-boy, recalls

> My mother and myself gazing down from our bedroom window at Isobel, who was speaking in the court below to the first of the arriving Stevensons. Bob was a dark, roughly dressed man as lithe and graceful as a Mexican *vaquero* (cowboy) and evoking something of the same misgiving.[6]

He was as eccentric in his dress as Louis. When he spoke to ladies there was often a mocking expression on his face, but he was very attractive to the fair sex. It would seem that Fanny was at first more attracted to 'Bob' than to Louis, for she wrote to her friend Timothy Rearden, an erudite lawyer, who was librarian in the Mercantile Bank in San Francisco, comparing Bob to 'Adonis' and 'Apollo' and praising his "wonderful grace", and his litheness. Bob, however, who had a mistress in Paris, was for a while attracted to Belle Osbourne rather than to her mother.

Belle was described by Birge Harrison, an American at Grez, as "a bewitching young girl of seventeen with eyes so large as to be out of drawing". Belle in her turn was in love with one of her many admirers, an Irish boy, Frank O'Meara. Nevertheless she was much intrigued with Louis. She said,

He never saw a real American girl before and he says I
act and talk as though I come out of a book - I mean an
American book. He is such a nice looking ugly man and
I would rather listen to him talk than read the most interesting book I ever saw. We sit in the little green arb-
our after dinner drinking coffee and talking till late at
night. Mama is ever so much better and getting prettier
every day.

She was the centre of attention, having hurt her ankle, so she lay
in a hammock while the others sprawled admiringly on the grass
around her.

It was all great fun at Grez for members of the artist colony,
the mad frolics on the river, the sports in which Louis took a leading part.

Little boys are often very observant. Lloyd Osbourne would
notice his mother and Louis engrossed in long conversation, while
the others were painting in the forest. As Louis had once been very
attentive to Frances Sitwell's little son at Cockfield Rectory, so
was he now to Lloyd, aged eight. He would play with Fanny Osbourne's son, reading him passages from *Pilgrim's Progress*. It is
likely that Lloyd in those early days began to hero-worship Louis,
and Fanny, too, must have observed his interest in her surviving
son. She took to painting the old bridge at Grez, her favourite study.

Will Low gives a picture of Louis,

his long fingers twisting cigarettes of thread-like dimen-
sions. I have never known anyone roll so thin a cigarette
as Stevenson and the constant flow of talk and inter-
change of thought come back to me like the opening
chapters of a book, which one has perused with increasing delight, only to find it at the end by a wilful convul-
sion of brute nature finished too soon.[7]

Low soon realized that his friend's apparent idleness was deceptive,
for he hid his industry. Though his books might remain unopened,
while staying in this idyllic setting, he was in reality gathering impressions of scenes and manners, a sort of industrious idleness. Low

52

wrote: "His mind was a treasure-house where every addition to its store was carefully guarded against the day of need." It was indeed a formative period.

While staying in these delightful French villages bordering Fontainebleau Forest, he was enriching his knowledge of fifteenth century French history, to be used later when he was writing his essays on 'François Villon, Student Poet and Housebreaker' and 'Charles of Orleans'. Stevenson was very fond of Montigny-sur-Loing where Low had a little house. He wrote in his essay on 'Fontainebleau Village Communities of Painters':

> Montigny has been somewhat strangely neglected. I never knew it inhabited, but once when Will H. Low installed himself there with a barrel of *Piquette* (light wine) and entertained his friends in a leafy trellis above the weir in sight of the green country and to the music of the falling water ... and from my memories of the place in general and that garden trellis in particular - at morning visited by birds, or at night when the dew fell and the stars were of the party - I am inclined to think perhaps too favourably of the future of Montigny.[8]

When Low on one occasion tucked R.L.S. in his bed after too bibulous a night out, he murmured, "How good you are, you remind me of my mother."

France was in every way a country very congenial to Louis. He loved a good bottle of Beaujolais-Fleury at 'Lavenue', the Paris restaurant, sipping it and saying, "I wish that we could get this in Edinburgh, for you don't know how I dread returning there and adapting myself to the ration of drink usual in the land of my fathers." He detested the intemperance that was common in Scotland.

One day during the autumn of 1876 Bob went for a long walk with Fanny in the forest and generously praised his cousin Louis, telling her she must cultivate her friendship with Louis.[9] "You must have nothing to say to *me*," he urged, "for I am only a vulgar cad, but Louis is a gentleman and you can trust him and depend on him." One habit of Louis perplexed Fanny. His emotional nature made him weep and throw himself upon the floor. She wrote to Tim Rearden:

When he begins to laugh, if he is not stopped in time, he
goes into hysterics, and has to have his fingers bent back
to bring him to himself again.[10]

Louis described Fanny as "Dark as a wayside gypsy, lithe as a
hedge-wood hare".

Many years later in an article in *The Century Magazine* (December 1916) Birge Harrison recalled the vivid impression Fanny
had made on him. He remembered,

> Her eyes of a depth and sombre beauty that I have never
> seen equalled - eyes, nevertheless, that upon occasion
> could sparkle with humour and brim over with laughter.
> Yet upon the whole Mrs. Osbourne impressed me as first
> of all a woman of profound character and serious judge-
> ment... But she belonged to the Quattro Century rather
> than to the nineteenth century. Had she been borne a
> Medici, she would have held rank as one of the remark-
> able women of all time.

Since Louis seemed so active at Grez, Fanny did not realize
at first that he suffered from bad health, but she soon suspected
that he was prone to tubercular illness. Exactly when they became
lovers will never be known, certainly not in those early days at Grez
when their friendship was developing, but later in Paris she was to
share his bed. Louis's sexual needs were very strong, but Fanny
had not yet decided on divorce proceedings against her husband.
Belle, many years later, refused to believe that her mother and
Louis were lovers before marriage,[11] for in the early days at least,
she adored her golden-bearded father Samuel Osbourne, being his
staunch partisan. Louis was ardently in love with Fanny and followed her, Lloyd and Belle to Paris.

There, during November 1876, he wrote one of the most sensitive of his essays, 'On Falling in Love', definitely inspired by his
love for Fanny Osbourne and, perhaps, the finest on the subject in
our language. In this essay, so replete with reflective wisdom, Stevenson shows that he is a true craftsman, influenced by the graceful
style of Charles Lamb, loving words for their own sake, and reveal-

ing sympathy, imagination and the understanding to explore the strange vagaries of human conduct.

"Falling in love," he wrote, "is the one illogical adventure, the one thing of which we are tempted to think as supernatural, in our trite and reasonable world..." "This simple accident of falling in love is as beneficial as it is astonishing. It arrests the petrifying influence of years, disproves cold-blooded and cynical conclusion and awakens dormant sensibilities." *The Cornhill Magazine* article varies rather from the article published in *Virginibus Puerisque*.

It is difficult to understand Frank Swinnerton's patronizing criticism of Stevenson as an essayist as "in the deepest sense unoriginal in delivering the judgements of a rather middle-aged inexperience." At twenty-six when he wrote 'On Falling in Love' he had plenty of mundane experience.

Stevenson's contemporary, Edmund Gosse thought R.L.S. primarily an essayist, "the best in my humble opinion," he wrote him, "(without one soul to approach you) since Lamb. To me you always seem an essayist writing stories rather than a born novelist."

Louis's intimacy with W.E. Henley deepened in 1876. Despite Henley's faults, his insensibility, his lack of tact and later, peevish jealousy of Stevenson, it is possible to forgive him when one bears in mind his tremendous courage and serenity during ill health, a bond between himself and Louis. Henley, a fine poet, little read today, once wrote to Stevenson, "The challenge of life lies not in the possible victory, but rather in the inevitable defeat." Henley really loved the image of his friend during the early Edinburgh days, "the old, riotous, intrepid, scornful Stevenson".[12] As his biographer relates, he could never forgive his friend for deserting, as he thought, the heroic anti-establishment struggle, owing to his later travels in America,[13] a country he despised for he was very insular. He never reconciled himself to Louis's marriage to Fanny, nor to his eventual travels to the South Seas. At the end of 1876, Henley left Edinburgh for London, where he was appointed editor of a weekly review called *London*. Henley lived in wretched lodgings in Shepherds Bush, and from time to time Louis gave him gifts or loans of money. Although Louis contributed essays, poems, and occasionally serial fiction to *London*, some of his friends, including Professor Fleeming Jenkin, disapproved of him prostituting his gifts by society journalism. In January 1878 Louis's story of the Brenner Pass, 'Will o' the Mill', was published by Leslie Stephen in the *Cornhill*. When Louis, in his Scottish accent, read it to Fanny and young Lloyd, she was full of enthusiasm, but it hardly ranks among his best writings.

Frances Sitwell, once so ardently loved, remained his intimate, trusted friend and even an intermediary with his father, but there was a subtle change in their relationship. It may well be that Fanny, aware of her lover's earlier sentiments for Mrs. Sitwell, influenced him to write less often to her. Louis had told Frances Sitwell about his affair with Fanny. In early 1877 - at least for three months - Louis was much in Edinburgh and in describing his slightly strained relations with his parents, he wrote Mrs. Sitwell: "I think I never feel so lonely as when I am too much with my father and mother, and I am ashamed of the feeling, which makes matters worse."

It is evident that Louis felt himself fully committed to Fanny some time before she returned to California. Not only had he a sense of moral commitment, but a sexual commitment. Although the situation was fraught with difficulty, for Fanny was still married to Sam Osbourne, Louis with his scrupulous sentiments towards women and his innate chivalry, was already considering the possibility of marriage with his lover. Meanwhile, he had confided in his father and mother, and may have even mentioned his desire to marry Fanny when she was free to do so. They were horrified. Thomas Stevenson visited Paris to see Louis, probably in order to obtain further information about the affair; but it is most unlikely that he met Fanny. It was easy for Louis to find many opportunities to visit her in Paris, but in the autumn of 1877 he became very ill with an eye infection, giving Fanny the chance to nurse him.

He was always a difficult invalid, so she decided to bring him to London for treatment. Whilst in London she made a favourable impression on Sidney Colvin and Frances Sitwell, who kindly asked her to stay in her house in Chepstow Place. Fanny was at first naturally ill at ease in London literary society.

She wrote to Timothy Rearden in America:

It seemed most incongruous to have the solemn Mr. Colvin, a Professor at Cambridge, and the stately, beautiful Mrs. Sitwell sit by me and talk in the most correct English about the progress of literature and the Arts. I was rather afraid of them, but they didn't seem to mind and came down to my level and petted me as one would stroke a kitten.[14]

Like Louis, she was fond of smoking, and he had warned her against this habit in Mrs. Sitwell's house, but she was most understanding about it, and even rolled cigarettes from Turkish tobacco together with Colvin. It was now that Fanny met Henley for the first time. Both Colvin and Mrs. Sitwell did their best to reconcile Louis with his parents and to stress Fanny's good character.

Thomas and Margaret Stevenson no doubt fervently hoped that with the passage of time the passion of their son for this married lady would be cured. They disapproved of his long absences in France, but at least in June 1878, Louis had a legitimate reason to reside in Paris, for he was temporarily employed as secretary to Professor Fleeming Jenkin, who was a juror at an international exhibition there.

By 1878 many of the great writers of the nineteenth century had died, Sir Walter Scott in 1832, Thackeray in 1863, and Dickens in 1870. Tennyson, however, was to live for another fourteen years and George Eliot (Mary Ann Cross) until 1880. Thomas Hardy and Henry James were alive, budding literary giants. In June, Louis received a very encouraging letter from Leslie Stephen, editor of *The Cornhill*, a constant friend.

It has occurred to me lately that you might help me in an ever recurring difficulty. I am constantly looking out rather vaguely for a new novelist. I should like to find a Walter Scott or Dickens, or even a Miss Bronte or G. Eliot. Somehow the coming man or woman has not yet been revealed. Meanwhile I cannot help thinking that if you would seriously put your hand to such a piece of work you would be able - I will not say to rival the success of *Waverley* or *Pickwick*, but to write something really good and able to make a mark in *The Cornhill*. Of course you must have thought of this, but a little push from outside may help the thought to develop itself. ... You might start a few chapters and then let me see whether I thought them available for *Cornhill* purposes. I have a strong persuasion that if a good subject struck your fancy, you could make a good piece of work.

This letter shows shrewd discernment and faith in Stevenson's future as a writer.

Colvin, always unselfish, and constantly ready to forward Stevenson's career, wrote to an editor from Trinity College Cambridge declining to write something about William Hazlitt[15] "owing to the multiplicity of literary engagements", but recommending Louis Stevenson, who "has been for some time looking for an opportunity to write about him."

Stevenson had enormous admiration for Hazlitt, writing to a friend during the autumn (1881), "You know I am a fervent Hazlittite", regarding him as *the* English writer who has had the scantiest justice. In his essay 'Walking Tours', both original and individualistic, Stevenson is obviously influenced by Hazlitt. He considered that a walking tour should be gone upon alone, because freedom is of the essence and quotes Hazlitt *On Going a Journey*: "I cannot see the wit of walking and talking at the same time. When I am in the country I wish to vegetate like the country." In 'Walking Tours' he wrote, "though we are mighty fine fellows nowadays, we cannot write like Hazlitt".

It is amusing that R.L.S. thought 'On Going on a Journey' so good that a tax should be levied on all who have not read it. In 1881, later in Switzerland, he even considered writing a biography of the great master and negotiated with a London publisher Bentley, but it proved abortive.

Partly reconciled to his parents, Louis spent Easter (1878) with them at Gairloch on the Clyde and again at Burford Bridge in England where he met George Meredith, then little appreciated by literary critics, but later to become an eminent novelist. Meredith, then aged fifty, was impressed by young Stevenson and congratulated him on *An Inland Voyage*, kindly assuring him: "The writing

58

is of the rare kind which is naturally simple yet picked and cho-ice."[16] They became friendly and often corresponded, for Steven-son almost excessively admired Meredith's work. Six years later he wrote Louis that he was finishing at a great pace, a two-volume novel to be called *Diana of the Crossways*. It is partly a portrait of Caroline Norton, granddaughter of Richard Brinsley Sheridan and a talented novelist and poetess in her own right.[17]

Stevenson had his experience of tardy editors, like many an-other author. He wrote to John Blackwood of the celebrated pub-lishing house in 1877[18]

> Dear Sir,
>   I regret to trouble you. But it would be an obligation if you could let me have the article of which you intend to make no use, either now or as soon as convenient.
>   Yours sincerely,
>   Robert Louis Stevenson

In another letter written from the Savile Club during 1878 Louis refers to "his paper" on 'The English Admirals', subsequently pub-lished in *Virginibus Puerisque*, asking the editor to return it to 17 Heriot Row. Montaigne's influence can surely be gleaned in this essay. Stevenson was writing about the heroes in our naval history, Sir Richard Grenville of the *Revenge*, that noted "tyrant to his crew, a dark bullying fellow", of Drake and Frobisher and Blake and Nelson, the greatest of them all.

Fanny was still in Paris during the early summer of 1878. There are indications that Louis was helping her with money, for Sam Osbourne only sent her irregular payments. Whether or not she was considering divorce at this stage is uncertain. She was un-easy about the reactions of her family, strict Presbyterians in In-dianapolis, to divorce and remarriage. For the lovers it was a time of crisis, fleeting days troubled by their problems and, what was worse, the uncertainty of not knowing if and when they would meet again. Fanny with Lloyd and Belle was about to return to America. Louis wrote to Baxter during June 1878, "This is the last twenty days of my passion. It will then be over for good."[19]

When Fanny returned to America in August, Louis was at the station to see her off. As he walked away he experienced a terrible loneliness.

VI

More Creative Endeavour

To obtain material for a new book Louis travelled to Le Monastier, situated in a highland valley near Le Puy, among the mountains of the Haute-Loire. "'Tis a mere mountain Poland," he wrote, "renowned for the making of lace, for drunkenness, for freedom of language and for its political dissension." There he spent a month, alone, preparing for his travels with a donkey in the Cévennes. The donkey named Modestine by Stevenson, cost him sixty-five francs and a bottle of brandy. She was the colour of a mouse with a kindly eye and a determined under-jaw.

The adventurous journey of eleven days undertaken by Louis and Modestine in the Cévennes resulted in his celebrated book, *Travels With A Donkey*, a work which will always appeal, especially to youth seeking adventure and wanderlust. In dedicating his book to Sidney Colvin, Louis wrote: "We are all travellers in what John Bunyan calls the wilderness of this world - all, too, travellers with a donkey, and the best that we find, in our travels is an honest friend." Before embarking on his journey, Stevenson had studied the history of the Camisards, for the precipitous and wild mountains of the Cévennes used to be their stronghold, and the rebels there had revolted against the French Government, from 1702 for about twelve years after the Edict of Nantes. They reminded Louis of his beloved Scottish Covenanters and their persecution by the English government.

It is a delightful book, with the radiance of Spring itself, though Louis undertook the journey in October, lyrical and musical in 'A Night Among the Pines', perhaps its best part. Modestine the donkey is so alive, tripping along upon her four small hoofs with a sober daintiness of gait. For several nights Louis slept out under the stars, "clear coloured and jewel-like" as he described them, listening to the sounds of the night and the barking of dogs. He missed Fanny awfully, betraying his longing for her in two memorable passages:

> And yet even while I was exulting in my solitude I became aware of a strange lack. I wished a companion to lie near me in the starlight, silent and not moving, but even within touch. For there is a fellowship more quiet even than solitude and which, rightly understood, is solitude made perfect and to live out of doors with the woman a man loves is of all lives the most complete and free.

Travels With A Donkey may not be either a gay or carefree book, for Louis without his Fanny felt an overwhelming sadness. Not enough has been written about his gaiety. Graham Balfour wrote:

> A child-like mirth leaped and danced in him, he seemed to skip upon the hills of life.

He was simply bubbling with quips and jests. Glee is a word one associates with Louis. "A solemn glee possessed my mind at this gradual and lovely coming in of day," he wrote. He was so sensitive and responsive to the wonders of nature and the spirit of life pervading everything and moving him to a strange exhilaration. How cherished was this out of door life.

> The blue darkness lay long in the glade where I had sweetly slumbered, but soon there was a broad streak of orange melting into gold along the mountain-tops of Vivarais.

In the country of the Camisards he suddenly hears a woman singing a sad ballad about love and a *bel amoureux*. It hurt Louis like a stab in the heart, reminding him of Fanny. "What could I have told her," wrote Louis,

Little enough, and yet all the heart requires. How the world gives and takes away, and brings sweethearts near, only to separate them again into distant and strange lands, but to love is the great amulet which makes the world a garden, and hope, which comes to all, outwears the accidents of life, and reaches with tremulous hand beyond the grave and death.

Life could be cruel to those in love.

Louis has little or no sympathy for Trappist monks, for he spent one night in the Trappist monastery of Our Lady of the Snows among the hills of Vivarais. For him the silent, contemplative life had no appeal, but he might have shown more understanding of those with a vocation for it. However, so often confined to a sick bed, he longed for a life of action. In his 'Our Lady of the Snows', a poem published in *Underwoods*, Louis wrote:

> O to be up and doing, O
> Unfearing and unashamed to go
> In all the uproar and the press
> About my human business.

Perhaps it was Cummy's and his father's influence that made him dislike the narrowness of vision of the monks.

> Aloof, unhelpful, and unkind,
> The prisoners of the iron mind,
> Where nothing speaks except the bell
> The unfraternal brothers dwell.

Louis would have agreed with the third verse of Emily Bronte's:

> No coward soul is mine.
> Vain are the thousand creeds
> That move men's hearts, unutterably vain.

Stevenson relates at the end of the journey how he wept when he had to sell Modestine "My lady friend, saddle and all" for thirty-five francs. He returned to London in the middle of October,

62

1878, to stay with Sidney Colvin in his rooms at Cambridge. He worked with such speed that the book was in proof by March 1879 and published in May by Kegan Paul.

His fourth essay, 'Truth of Intercourse'[1], is influenced by the misunderstandings that had clouded the relations between himself and his parents, and by his love for Fanny Osbourne. "To speak truth," Louis wrote,

> there must be moral equality or else no respect; and hence between parent and child, intercourse is apt to degenerate into fencing bout, and misapprehensions to become ingrained.

The parent began with an imperfect notion of the child's character, formed in early years or during the equinoctial gales of youth.

> In the closest of all relations, that of a love well founded and equally shared - speech is half discarded, like a roundabout, infantile process or a ceremony of formal etiquette, and the two communicate directly by their presences, and with few looks and fewer words contrive to share their good and evil and uphold each other's hearts in joy.

Louis's sentiments towards Edinburgh were ambivalent, he both loved it and hated it, particularly its climate, but he knew his native city intimately and describes it lovingly in *Edinburgh Picturesque Notes*, first published in articles in *The Portfolio* from June to December 1878 and later in book form in *Fleet Street*. It was his second book to be published in that year, because *An Inland Voyage* had appeared earlier. There are chapters about Carlton Hill with its views of Edinburgh Castle and Arthur's Seat, Greyfriars and Stevenson's beloved Pentlands, perhaps the best part of his book.

> Far out in the lowlands Edinburgh shows herself making a great smoke on clear days and spreading her suburbs about her for miles ... a crying hill-bird, the bleat of a sheep, a wind singing in the dry grass, seem not so much

to interrupt, as to accompany the stillness, but to the spiritual ear the whole scene makes a music at once human and rural, and discourses pleasant reflections on the destiny of man.

It is unfortunate that Stevenson never published an essay on his favourite poet of Edinburgh, Robert Fergusson, though he planned one. "There is a kind of gaping admiration," he wrote in *Edinburgh Picturesque Notes*[2],

> that would fain roll Shakespeare and Bacon into one, to have a bigger thing to gape at, and a class of man who cannot edit one author without disparaging all others. They are indeed mistaken if they think to please the great originals, and whoever puts Fergusson right with fame, cannot do better than dedicate his labours to the memory of Burns, who will be best delighted of the dead.

The autumn of 1878 was a busy, creative time for Louis, engrossed in his *Pavilion on the Links*, in which he shows his craftsmanship. It is an exciting story, though criticized by Colvin, but later accepted for publication by Leslie Stephen. It was now that Stevenson and Henley began to collaborate in the writing of plays, but Stevenson had no real gift for writing for the theatre. Both authors were buoyed up by false hopes that they would make a great deal of money in these ventures into the world of drama. Stevenson had always been fascinated by the dual character of Deacon (William) Brodie, a respected Edinburgh cabinet-maker in the latter part of the eighteenth century in daytime and at night, leader of a gang of criminal burglars in Edinburgh and its environs in 1787. Deacon had a grim end. After being betrayed by an accomplice, he tried to escape to America, but was arrested in Amsterdam, brought back to Edinburgh to be tried and hung in 1788.

Louis saw a great deal of W.E. Henley during the winter of 1878, going to his friend's house in Shepherds Bush to collaborate on the play. In London, Louis went much to the Savile - he was a member there for twenty years - and wrote to his mother from there on March 19th 1875. He had been visiting the Stephens - the helpful editor of *The Cornhill* and his wife. He alludes to a visit to Paris (before he knew Fanny). "I am in a French hotel," he wrote, "French bread, French waiters, French absence of soap in bedrooms and general Frenchiness even to most curious and unpleasant details." Very rarely did he criticize France.

Louis was excellent company at the club, amusing a fellow member, Herbert Spencer, in the Billiards Room at 107 Piccadilly[3] when he remarked: "Proficiency at billiards is the sign of an illspent youth." Full of enthusiasm, Louis and Henley worked on *Deacon Brodie* at Swanston. When staged, however, at Bradford in December 1882, and later in Aberdeen and the Prince's Theatre in London, it was not a success, nor did it attract large audiences when Henley's young brother Teddy, addicted to drink, took the leading part in America.

An important essay, already alluded to, 'Some Aspects of Robert Burns', was first rejected by *The Encyclopaedia Britannica* for being too unorthodox and heretical. Then Leslie Stephen asked Louis to write a piece about Burns for *The Cornhill*, which was completed during the summer of 1879 and later reprinted in *Familiar Studies of Men and Books*. Stevenson condemns Burns too sternly for his sordid affair with Jean Armour, the mother of his bastard children. It may have been in a mood of self-flagellation, scourging himself as a fellow Bohemian, while he criticized Scotland's national poet. Later Stevenson regretted his condemnation, writing: "Now I knew for my own part, that it was with the profoundest pity, but with a growing esteem, that I studied the man's desperate efforts to do right." What he really deplored was his omission to state this more noisily. To criticize too strongly Scotland's national poet was bound to land him in trouble.

Earlier, Stevenson had written his essay on 'Charles of Orleans' having acquired a keen interest in French history and literature during his sojourn at Barbizon. Charles was the son of Louis de Valois, Duke of Orleans, brother to King Charles VI. Stevenson mentions Queen Isabella, the child-widow of Richard II, murdered in Pontefract Castle. In 1406 she was married to Charles of Orleans, and would often relate to him the melancholy story of Richard's life, and her own life was sad, for she died in 1409. Charles would never forget Richard's fate, *"ce mauvais cas"* - that ugly business must be avenged, he wrote. In 1415 he was taken prisoner at Agincourt and incarcerated for many years, not without mitigation, in Windsor Castle and the Tower of London.

Stevenson had a poor opinion of Charles of Orleans as a poet, though he appreciated his rondels. Yet his verses were graceful, and Stevenson considered that he was very much more of a Duke in his verses than in his absurd and inconsequential career as a statesman when released from prison and returned to France. This essay was published in *The Cornhill* during December 1876.

Bohemian characters always attracted R.L.S. and it is not surprising that he wrote an essay on François Villon, the fifteenth century French poet, born in Paris in 1431, the same year that Joan of Arc was burnt at the stake in Rouen. The popular conception of Villon is of a romantic character, idolized by the *canaille* of Paris. In such a way did he appear in *The Vagabond King*, a musical play, staged during the early nineteen-thirties in London. Stevenson, usually the realist, was no sentimentalist, but in his portrait of Villon he is too much of a moralist. As he wrote in the preface[4], he could only see "artistic evil" in Villon, where others might find beautiful and human traits. Was he once more flagellating himself, feeling a little remorse for his own bohemianism in the Edinburgh underworld of his youth? His judgment is too harsh, for he does not make sufficient allowance for Villon's poverty and the circumstances in which he was born. If Villon was a truant when young and he admits to it, so was Stevenson and he might be expected to be more tolerant of Villon's frailties on this score. However, there is much to admire in his essay, though Villon's career is obscure. He was both professional robber and guilty of savage brawls. Stevenson's ultimate verdict is that,

> François was a sinister dog in all likelihood, but with a look in his eye, and the loose flexile mouth that goes with wit and an overweening sensual temperament. Certainly the sorriest figure on the rolls of fame.

Stevenson also wrote a short story about Villon called *A Lodging for the Night*, a tale praised by some, but somewhat artificial.

It was fortunate for Louis to have so much work to distract his mind, for he was in a highly nervous state by the summer of 1879, anxious about Fanny in California. He could not be at all certain that she might not return to her husband. If he had known that after her return to California, she had experienced a breakdown or mental collapse, he would have been even more anxious. Separated from Fanny for about a year, Louis's physical needs were very urgent. J.A. Steuart, one of his biographers, relates that while absent from her, Louis had two amorous affairs with attractive women. One was with the brunette daughter of an Aberdeen builder and carpenter working in Edinburgh. The other woman, in complete contrast, was tall and fair, the daughter of a Midlothian blacksmith.[5] These deadly rivals competing for Louis's attentions are alleged to have indulged in a terrible scene when physical violence occurred near Swanston Cottage while Louis was staying with his parents. Though one may suspect that such a colourful story was fictitious, it could bear some truth. He was always frank about his own emotional weaknesses.

Nellie Vandegrift Sanchez in the life of her sister[6], mentions that Fanny was very much run down in health in California, but she is silent about her mental breakdown. She hesitated about starting proceedings for divorce against her husband Sam, blowing hot and cold over it. She needed peace and quiet, and found it in a sleepy old Mexican town with a strong Spanish influence in California, named Monterey, then completely unspoilt. Fanny, reared in the country, an expert horsewoman and gypsy-like, joined a party of friends accompanying a party of *vaqueros* (cowboys) in a rodeo (cattle round-up) on a San Francisco ranch near Monterey. Gradually she recovered her health in the open-air life, riding through a picturesque countryside of redwoods where the delicious gurgle of fresh mountain streams could be heard in the scented air.

It is unfortunate that we have no letters from Fanny to Louis while they were absent from one another. Nor do we know the contents of her extremely urgent cable to her lover received by him towards the end of July 1879. Louis immediately decided to leave for America, going to London on July 30th. Before leaving Edinburgh he bought a ticket for New York at the Anchor Steamship Line in Hanover Street. In refraining from telling his parents about his proposed precipitous journey, Louis lays himself open to the charge of callousness or even cowardice. Perhaps he was afraid to tell them, supposing that they might try to deter him or prevent him going. He merely told them that he was travelling on business. It was natural for them to resent his sudden journey because they were expecting him to accompany them to a spa abroad where Thomas Stevenson wanted to drink the waters.

Louis, however, did confide in his intimate friends, and they all attempted to influence him not to undertake the journey. In their opinion it was a mad venture. He was an egoist, but what a grand gesture on his part to embark on this uncertain, dangerous journey. It reveals how deeply he loved Fanny. Thomas Stevenson greatly agitated, wrote to Colvin, whom he liked, imploring him to use his influence on Louis to induce him not to go. "Is it fair that we should be half-murdered by his conduct?" he wrote. "I see nothing but destruction to himself as well as to all of us." Where he had formerly blamed Bob for unsettling his son's faith, he now condemned Herbert Spencer, a fellow author and a favourite companion in the billiard room at the Savile.

Colvin feared for Louis's health, telling him that "if the spirit will go playing fast and loose with its body, the body will some day decline the association and we shall be left without our friend." For his part, Henley argued that it was folly for Louis to go to America when he should stay in England to woo Stephen and other editors to give him work. He appealed to his ambition. As Louis prowled restlessly about the room, smoking a cigarette, looking thin and emaciated, Gosse made valiant efforts to dissuade his friend from going on "the maddest of enterprises". It was to no avail. Louis would brook no obstacle and was determined to leave. He paid £8 for his passage to New York.

It was August 7th 1879, a momentous day when Henley came to the station to say farewell in the Glasgow train from St. Pancras. Louis left on the *S.S. Devonia,* sailing down the Clyde, and just before departure wrote a note to his father, enclosed in a letter to Colvin. To Bob, he wrote that Fanny had been very ill, and that he hoped to get her to do one of two things. "At least if I fail in my great purpose, I shall see some wild life in the West," he added. To Baxter he confided that he was in fair spirits, "a little off my head and off my food". He was in a subterranean smoking room, and a barmaid was not far off, waiting.

68

VII

By Second Cabin to America

In order to travel by 'second cabin' to America, rather than by steerage, Louis had to pay two guineas more. The steerage fare was six guineas, but he explains in *The Amateur Emigrant*, an account of his travel experiences, that although anxious to see the worst of emigrant life, he needed a table for his writing. A 'second cabin' passenger had many advantages over a 'steerage' passenger. Whereas a 'steerage' passenger would have to bring his own bedding or dishes, a 'second cabin' passenger found berths and a roughly furnished table. The food, too, was rather better by 'second cabin', than by 'steerage', though porridge was common to both classes, and the dinner of soup, fresh roast beef, boiled salt junk and potatoes eaten by both categories of passengers. However, the mere chicken bones and flakes of lukewarm fish do not sound very appetising. Louis was in the habit of eating plenty of porridge, bread and soup throughout the ten day journey and before turning in, consoled himself with some whisky, water and a few biscuits.

One of the most admirable traits in Stevenson's character was his complete absence of snobbery, his ability to mix freely with all manner of people. He loathed class distinctions, deploring their strict observance in England. "Ladies?" he once said to a visitor when he was living later in Bournemouth, "One of the truest ladies in Bournemouth, Mrs. Watts, is at this moment cleaning my study windows."[1]

As a writer, Louis was passionately interested in his fellow human beings, and liked nothing better than to walk on the deck with another passenger named Jones, a blacksmith from Wales, dissecting "our neighbours in a spirit that was too purely scientific to be called unkind". As a shrewd character study of the men and women Stevenson encountered on the *Devonia*, *The Amateur Emigrant* is a massive achievement, but less satisfactory, perhaps, when considered as narrative. His keen observation never played him false, his picture, for instance, of an Irish-American, for all the world like a beggar in a print by Callot, one-eyed, with great, splay, crow's feet round the sockets; a knotty squat nose coming down over his moustache, a miraculous hat; a shirt that had been white, ay, ages long ago ... no buttons to his trousers.[2]

One thing Louis fiercely resented was the patronizing visit of first-class saloon passengers, drawn by curiosity to the steerage, where they gazed on the passengers as if they were passing through a menagerie.

So Louis, despite some privations, passed the duration of the ten day voyage not unpleasantly, and certainly most profitably. Stevenson worked hard, managing to complete, despite the difficulties, his tale 'The Story of a Lie', a work begun during the previous July in Scotland. Dick Naseby, the main character, is alleged to be a self-portrait of Stevenson himself and old Squire Naseby is probably a portrait of his father Thomas. It is curious how the uneasy relationship between father and son is of such importance in his books. Louis sent it to Colvin, who succeeded in getting it published in *The New Quarterly*. Louis was far from idle, working on copious notes for *The Amateur Emigrant*, a book completed later in San Francisco.

Stevenson, with his customary friendliness, mixed freely among the cosmopolitan emigrants, comprised of gloomy Scots, English, Irish, Germans, Scandinavians and one Russian. The *Devonia* was not full of lusty, enterprising youths afire with enthusiasm, but mainly middle-aged people "broken by adversity, eager to set foot in America". The pitching and the rolling of the ship would not have troubled Louis, for he loved the sea.

To the officers, the doctor, the purser, and the stewards, Louis was an oddity, spending most of his time writing. One day the purser came to see him, and doubtless thinking he was wasting his time "by my misguided industry", offered him paid work if he was to copy out the list of passengers.

Only in one respect was Louis's vanity pricked. In normal circumstances he was accustomed to many a glance from members of the fair sex, but travelling by 'second cabin' he found that every woman passed him like a dog".

This was Stevenson's first visit to New York. When he arrived on August 18th it was pouring with rain so that his impressions were very dismal. He relates his nightmare wanderings in torrents of rain to banks, post-offices, money-changers, railway-officers, publishers and booksellers. Louis found both rudeness and amazing kindness among many of the Americans he encountered. One moment they may be insulting a stranger, the next moment loading him with attention. On this inauspicious first visit, Louis saw very little of New York, but he was to learn to know and love America. A favourite place for him was Washington Square where on other visits he enjoyed talking to and playing with the children. He once passed an afternoon there with Mark Twain, according to Fanny, his future wife. Stevenson's night in New York was at a very humble lodging, the abode of an Irishman named Mitchell, and he was obliged to sleep on the floor because the only bed was occupied by somebody off the boat.

Now began for Louis the nightmare emigrant train journey, described so graphically in *Across the Plains*. At dusk Louis made for the ferry station, fairly heavily loaded with a valise, a knapsack and six tomes of George Bancroft's *History of the United States*, somehow packed into the pockets of his travelling bag. The ferry station was fearfully overcrowded with a mass of seething humanity all crossing the river by ferry to Jersey City and then a long, exhausting wait for the train. For Louis, a sick man, numb with cold, the train journey was a terrible ordeal. Louis relates in *Across the Plains* about his landing in Jersey:

> A panic selfishness, like that produced by fear, presided over the disorder of our landing. People pushed, and elbowed and ran, their families following how they could. Children fell, and were picked up to be rewarded by a blow.... I sat on my valise, too crushed to observe my neighbours; but as they were all cold, and wet, and weary, and driven stupidly crazy by the mismanagement to which we had been subjected, I believe they can have been no happier than myself.

Except for some oranges (only two of them had the pretence of juice)[3], Louis had nothing to eat for thirty hours. He found it almost impossible to sleep except by taking laudanum. Since he felt ill and feverish, suffered from diarrhoea, and probably from dysentery, the oppressive odour from unwashed bodies and the primitive lavatory conditions made matters worse. Yet he took pleasure in the names of the states and territories he travelled through: Delaware, Ohio, Indiana, Florida, Dakota, and Susquehanna. Louis exalted in the beauty of Susquehanna, a river he had first seen at sunrise. He called it "that shining river and desirable valley". Louis had taught himself to write under the most difficult conditions, when travelling by boat, on a railway platform, or on a train. In later life he sometimes wrote in bed. Now remembering with emotion the beauty of Susquehanna, and as the emigrant train wended its way through plains rich with corn where graceful trees framed the landscape, Louis wrote a melancholy note to Colvin, enclosing a poem which was subsequently published. It is about Susquehanna. Here is the first verse:

> Of where and how, I nothing know,
> And why I do not care,
> Enough, if even so,
> My travelling eyes, my travelling mind can go
> By flood and field and hill, by wood and meadow
> > fair,
> Beside the Susquehanna and along the Delaware.

Louis made many contacts on the train, just as he had done on the *Devonia*, with Dutch widows and with newsboys, great personages on American trains, selling all kinds of things, such as fruit, lollipops, papers, tea, coffee and sugar. The newsboys varied in character. One was "a dark, bullying, contemptuous, insolent scoundrel" much disliked by the travellers on the train, while another, a kindly lad, could not have been more helpful. On one occasion, when Louis was holding the door of his car open with his foot, gasping for air, for he felt very ill, the newsboy struck his foot aside, but as if to make amends a little later, having observed that Louis was looking ill, he gave him a large juicy pear.

72

Always there was Stevenson's invincible curiosity about his fellow humans, and his zest for their companionship. Dog-tired when he reached Chicago, a great city, but a gloomy one, and feeling hot and feverish, Louis sat on a bench while a little German gentleman poured out stories of pickpockets on the train. However ill he felt, he was nearly always a good listener.

Louis's complete lack of snobbery made him friends on the train, but neither Colvin nor Henley approved of *The Amateur Emigrant* or its second part, *Across the Plains*. Indeed they both objected to these works strongly, deeming them below R.L.S.'s usual standard. It is very probable that Victorian middle-class prejudices prevailing in 1879 were responsible for these far from flattering opinions of *The Amateur Emigrant* and its fellow. Frankly Louis's cultured friends in London did not approve of his egalitarianism, his readiness to become friendly with his working-class companions on boat or train. His father abhorred *The Amateur Emigrant*, particularly disliking the passage where Stevenson criticizes the first-class passengers for gaping at the steerage families as if they were a menagerie. It is a little more difficult to understand Henley's view of the book, for as a rebel, too, against Victorian values, he might be expected to appreciate Stevenson's aims. However, he was strongly opposed to Louis's quixotic travel to America from the beginning. Stevenson's account of the emigrant train journey, *Across the Plains*, was first published in an abridged form, four years after the journey in *Longman's Magazine* (1883). Nine years later, it was reprinted together with a shortened version of *The Amateur Emigrant*, called *From the Clyde to Sandy Hook*.

Louis was near the end of his arduous journey across the plains. On the afternoon of August 29th he had reached Sacramento in California, the city of gardens, and on the following day, before dawn, the train stopped on the Oakland side of San Francisco Bay. He wrote:

> The day was breaking as we crossed the ferry: the fog was rising over the citied hills of San Francisco; the bay was perfect - not a ripple, scarce a stain, upon its blue expanse, everything was waiting, breathless for the sun ... the air seemed to awaken, and began to sparkle; and

suddenly ... the city of San Francisco, and the bay of gold and corn, were lit from end to end with summer daylight.[4]

Fanny was now staying in Monterey, a quiet coastal town, very Spanish and Mexican in its way of life. It lay 130 miles south of San Francisco. Fanny, together with Lloyd and Belle and her sister Nellie Vandegrift, soon to marry a charming young man of Spanish nationality, Adolfo Sanchez of Monterey, a handsome bartender, was staying with a Mexican lady, Senorita Maria Bonifacio[5], known to her friends as Dona Nachita. Though Fanny's relations with Sam Osbourne were very strained, she was still seeing him at weekends, and they were not yet divorced.

Hastening to join her, Louis travelled by the Southern Pacific railroad as far as Salinas and then by railway to Monterey. When Louis arrived at the house where Fanny was staying, she was very happy to see him, though Lloyd, now eleven, an observant little boy, noticed how ill Louis was looking, his face gaunt, his body emaciated, and his clothes shabby - only his eyes shone with their strange, brilliant light. "Lully's coming," Fanny told her son, and Lloyd was thrilled at the announcement. Louis's arrival indeed came at a very awkward time for Fanny, not least because Belle was giving her much worry, having recently eloped with a penniless young San Franciscan artist, Joe Strong, whom she secretly married. Belle's father encouraged the match, but Fanny was opposed to it. On her part, Belle was rather hostile to Louis at this period, later relating in her autobiography,

> Maybe my mother saw in this contrast to my father the security from infidelity that had wrecked their marriage ... I ... had no hope she would not marry this penniless foreigner.[6]

She was only to become intimate with him years later in Samoa. One quandary perplexing Fanny's mind was whether Louis on his uncertain income and strained relations with his parents could possibly maintain her as his wife. Was there any real need, however, for her to write earlier to her lawyer friend, Timothy Rearden, in San Francisco with a distortion of the truth to say that her literary friend from Scotland had been invited to come to America on a lecture tour?

According to Nellie Sanchez, Louis's future sister-in-law, he was fond of good food and was especially partial to some delectable "little cakes", smoking-hot backing-powder biscuits, and when their Chinese cook Ah-Sing put them on the table, Louis was very happy. In Monterey, Louis, Fanny and Nellie would sometimes go to Jules Simoneau's restaurant, which specialized in moderately priced excellent French and Spanish cookery. Simoneau was fifty-eight, a cheery, good-hearted soul, who had once been a wealthy Nantais tradesman. He was to prove a staunch friend to R.L.S. According to Nellie, Simoneau's wife Dona Martina, a native of Miraflores in Lower California, cooked especially well *Tamales* made of corn-meal and chopped meat rolled in cornhusks and boiled. Another favourite dish was chilli con carne , a stew of meat and red peppers.

In Monterey Louis lived in a simple, but pleasant adobe house. He loved to walk on the beach either alone or with Fanny and Nellie, listening to the roar of the great waves beating on the Pacific shores. It inspired his work 'Monterey the Old Pacific Capital', first printed in *Fraser's Magazine* (November 1880) and reprinted in *Across the Plains* (1892). There Louis could watch the sand-pipers "trot in and out by troops after the return'g waves, trilling together in a chorus of infinitesimal song". The bones of whales or even the whole carcase of a whale lying scattered on the beach made an eerie impression. Stevenson's affinity with the sea can be grasped when he writes:

> The waves come in slowly, vast and green, curve their translucent necks, and burst with a surprising uproar, that runs, waxing and waning, up and down the long keyboard of the beach...

Recalling the vivid scene some time later, Louis would write verses *To My Name-Child*.[7] This was Louis, the son of Nellie Sanchez and her husband Adolpho.

The woodlands, too, enticed Louis, haunted as it seemed to him by the thundering surges, and the solitary Mexican, dark and smiling, with his axe, only interested in his straying cattle.

Louis was working hard at his writing in Monterey, later finishing 'The Pavilion on the Links', and starting his essay on 'Henry David Thoreau', the American author and naturalist. This work is one of Stevenson's best, now published in *Men and Books*. For some reason or other he never completed his *A Vendetta in the West*, an adventure story. Sometimes he would read aloud to Fanny and Nellie from some French author, and during his stay in Monterey he wanted to study Spanish with Nellie.

When Fanny returned to a cottage at Oakland to settle her divorce with her husband, Louis remained at Monterey, but he felt desolate and very lonely without her. There is no doubt that she loved Louis, but she was worried about her parents in Indiana and their reaction to a divorce. Louis confided in Charles Baxter, a steadfast friend in all his troubles. In October he wrote him a letter not mentioning his own wretched health, but Fanny's maladies.

> I have not only got Fanny patched up again in health, but the effect of my arrival has straightened out everything. As now arranged there is to be a private divorce in January after the girls are married (Nellie married Adolfo Sanchez of Monterey and Belle married Joseph Strong), and yours truly will himself be a married man as soon thereafter as the law and decency permit.[8]

In Scotland, Baxter was in charge of Louis's finances, and on several occasions sent him money, for Louis was desperately in need of it. Earlier he had hired a horse and camped in the Santa Lucia mountains above Monterey, but he had fallen seriously ill, so that for two days he lay beneath a pine-tree in a dazed state barely able to stagger to fetch water from a stream for himself and his horse. He might have died had not two frontiersmen found him and brought him back to their ranch where they nursed him, but his recovery in health was very slow.

In England, Edmond Gosse and his many friends missed Stevenson awfully. Gosse wrote to Louis in December from 29, Delamere Terrace, knowing how desperately ill his friend was: "Come straight back to us from that Monterey. Whether you live or die you will live for ever in our hearts and in the roll of men of genius." To a friend Hamo Thornycroft, Gosse confided:

> He (R.L.S.) does not think he will recover.... He is a charming creature, all instinct with genius and power. He is absolutely one of the best prose-writers we possess, he has but to die and people will at once say "the best". He is exactly like Hamlet's description of Yorick - "a fellow of infinite jest, of most excellent fancy".[9]

Gosse thought that Louis possessed the ardent, restless temperament of John Keats. Perhaps Stevenson felt a fellow feeling for Gosse, for both authors experienced very complicated relations with their fathers. Louis later considered Gosse's life of his father, "a very delicate task very delicately done".

Louis became very fond of Monterey. At the time he sojourned there the town was "essentially and wholly Mexican", and it has not lost that flavour even today, though greatly changed. He was sensitive to its romance, liking to lie awake while a Mexican would sing a love-song to the accompaniment of his guitar in the soft, caressing air. However, he foresaw the evil commercialism, soon to vanquish the quaint old ways. "Alas for the little town", he finished his essay on Monterey.

> It is not strong enough to resist the influence of the flaunting caravanserai, and the poor, quaint, penniless native gentlemen of Monterey must perish, like a lower race, before the millionaire vulgarians of the Big Bonanza.

Louis worked hard in his room in Girardin's lodging house, known today as Stevenson House[10], a flourishing museum in Alvarado Street, named after a lieutenant of Hernando Cortez, the Spanish adventurer. For meals he would resort to Simoneau's restaurant, frequented by Italian fishermen, Spaniards and cosmopolitans. Louis was so impoverished that some of his friends clubbed together two dollars a week for his upkeep, but he thought that he was earning the money from articles he contributed to the local newspaper, *The Monterey Californian*.

On December 18th 1879, Fanny at last obtained her decree of divorce against her husband Sam. However, her marriage to Louis was delayed for some months, partly because her widowed mother had not been told and did not approve of divorce. He was about to rejoin his beloved in San Francisco when illness struck at him, a bout of pleurisy. In mid-December he was well enough, however, to leave Monterey for San Francisco, but he thought often of death, despite his bravery and gaiety. He wrote to Gosse:

> Death is no bad friend; a few aches and gasps, and we are done, like the truant child. I am beginning to grow weary and timid in this big jostling city, and could run to my nurse, even although she should have to whip me before putting me to bed.

About now he wrote the first draft of his poem 'The Requiem', while he lay in the shadow of death. Here is the first verse:

> Under the wide and starry sky
> Dig the grave and let me lie.
> Glad did I live, and gladly die,
> And I laid me down with a will.

Louis felt a tremendous wave of optimism about 'the great new nation' America,[11] as he described her in little known verses, written in San Francisco.

> See the great new nation
>   New spirit and new scope
> Rise there from the sea's round shoulder
>   A splendid sun of hope.

Yet he had reservations. "America tread softly," he wrote "you bear the fruit of years".

VIII

Marriage to Fanny

In San Francisco where Louis was to spend the next six months, he had a modest, one room apartment in a house, 608 Bush Street, leased by an Irish family named Carson. A plaque tells us that Robert Louis Stevenson lodged there from December 1879-March 1880. Fanny and Nellie, not much older than Fanny's daughter Belle, were still staying in the little house across the bay at Oakland, described by R.L.S. in the dedication to *Prince Otto* as "far gone in the respectable stages of antiquity". The first rough draft of *Prince Otto* was written in San Francisco, a novella influenced by the style of George Meredith.

Christmas 1879 was a forlorn, lonely time for Louis. He wrote to Colvin on December 26th: "I am writing you in a café waiting for some music to begin. For four days I have spoken to no one but to my landlady or landlord or to restaurant waiters...". Since Sam Osbourne had lost his job, Louis had not only to keep himself, but maintain Fanny in her cottage in East Oakland. Occasionally he would lunch well at Donadieu's Restaurant, but he mostly lived very frugally, eating rolls and drinking coffee.

Louis corresponded with Gosse, on January 23rd (1880), calling him "My dear and kind Weg", a nickname used because Gosse, after a temporary spell of lameness, reminded him of Silas Wegg, the literary gentleman with a wooden leg in *Our Mutual Friend*. "I am now engaged to be married," he wrote, "to the woman whom I have loved for three and a half years ... I do not think many wives are better loved than mine will be."[1] To Professor Meiklejohn, a fellow Scot and fellow member of the Savile Club: "I am glad you like Burns." He mentions a paper he has written on the Japanese patriot, Yoshida-Torajiro, a man of many parts, an essay accepted by Leslie Stephen for *The Cornhill* and later included in *Men and Books*.

Neither Colvin nor Henley gave Stevenson any real encouragement at this time, tending to disparage his work, and to blame his sorry plight on his own rash venture. Henley feared that nothing could be done to prevent Louis from marrying Fanny Osbourne. Of his friends, Charles Baxter gave Louis constant support, and without it Louis would have been unable to prolong his stay in California. On January 26th he admitted to Baxter: "I have to drop from a 50 cent to a 25 cent dinner, today begins my fall. That brings down my outlay in food and drink to 45 cents, or 1/10½ per day."

Then during March Louis experienced further trouble, an all-pervading sadness caused by the dangerous illness of the four-year old son of his landlady. He had sat up with the feverish little boy through long nights and devotedly cared for him. He wrote to Colvin from 608 Bush Street: "And O, what he has suffered! O never, never any family for me! I am cured of that." The boy recovered, but Louis succumbed to more illness, an attack of malaria. His lungs were very weak and he suffered from mental fatigue and lack of sufficient food. About this time he experienced his first haemorrhage, and for the remainder of his life he was constantly menaced by the risk of further haemorrhages.

Suddenly and unexpectedly Louis received a cable from his father during April, saying he was willing to provide him with an allowance of two hundred and fifty pounds a year. It seems probable that Charles Baxter had interceded on Louis's behalf with his parents, and Thomas Stevenson, formerly opposed to his son's marriage and realizing that he could not prevent it, generously offered him the money. Louis was deeply grateful to his father. To Colvin, Louis wrote: "My Dear People telegraphed me in these words 'Count on £250 annually'."

He now moved into the Oakland Cottage to stay with Fanny and Nellie, to be devotedly nursed by Fanny. For six weeks Louis relates:

> It was a toss-up for life or death, on the verge of a galloping consumption, cold sweats, prostrating attacks of cough, sinking fits in which I lost the power of speech, fever, and all the ugliest circumstances of the disease.

80

Nellie, however, describes Louis's "boyish gaiety" even when sick, his fondness for teasing Fanny and herself by talking broad Scots "by the hour" while a whimsical smile lit up his expressive, brown eyes. He recovered from his illness, and as a celebration, he escorted Fanny and Nellie to Gilbert and Sullivan's *The Pirates of Penzance*.

Nellie relates that Stevenson's favourite songs of America were *Marching Through Georgia* and *Dixie*, but he never cared for *Home Sweet Home* on the grounds that "it made too brutal an assault upon a man's tenderest feelings".

Louis was, at this period, haunted by the dread of premature death when he knew that most of his best work had yet to be written. Such thoughts assailed him, and it was a release to turn them into poetry:

> Alas, not yet thy human task is done!
> A bond at birth is forged, a debt doth lie
> Immortal on mortality....
> Leave not, my soul, the unfoughten field, nor leave
> Thy debts dishonoured, nor thy place desert
> Without due service rendered. For thy life
> Up, spirit and defend that fort of clay,
> Thy body, now beleaguered.[2]

Stevenson was capable of writing good poetry. He would have agreed with Lord Alfred Douglas, rather underrated today, though he wrote at least several great sonnets: "Good poetry is the result of intense and violent effort, though the finished article shows no sign at all of the struggle it took to produce it."[3]

Fanny's surpassing gift to her Louis was her profound faith in his genius at a time of considerable mental conflict in his mind when even he was assailed by doubts. However, the future would show that her influence on his work was both beneficial and harmful. Her sister relates that Fanny married Louis when his fortunes, both in health and finances, were at their lowest ebb, but she refrains from mentioning that Fanny's health was by no means strong and that she suffered from breakdowns and neuroses. Louis's own precarious health had deteriorated owing to the privations he had endured in pursuing her.

In his writings[4], Louis provides a memorable picture of the San Francisco he knew:

> The air is fresh and salt as if you were at sea. On the one hand is Oakland gleaming white among its gardens. On the other, to seaward, hill after hill is crowded and crowned with the palaces of San Francisco... the town is essentially not Anglo-Saxon, still more essentially not American... For we are free in that city of gold to which adventurers congregated out of all the winds in heaven... There goes the Mexican unmistakable; there the blue-clad Chinaman with his white slippers.... You hear French, German, Italian, Spanish and English indifferently....

Stevenson, always the observer, would go to sit upon a bench in Portsmouth Square where he listened to the stories of the down-and-outs who came there. In *The Wrecker* Stevenson makes use of his knowledge of San Francisco, fascinated by the light and colour around Portsmouth Square, "the small eating-shops, transported bodily from Genoa or Naples with their macaroni and Chianti flasks and portraits of Garibaldi and coloured political caricatures". Above all, the thousand eccentricities of Chinatown attracted him, the multi-racial atmosphere and its ambiguities seeming to one of his character as of a vitalized museum. Later in the South Seas he similarly would make use of his contacts with shady characters to write his story of adventure, *The Ebb-Tide*.

One of his favourite walks was up Telegraph Hill, formerly known as "Signal Hill", with its grass-ground streets, the abode of Italians and other Latin peoples.

Among Fanny's and Louis's friends in San Francisco were the Virgil Williamses, staunch allies, who gave them constant support in the difficult days before their marriage. Two years later Louis told Henley in a letter, "Mrs. W was my guardian angel and our Best Man and Bridesmaid rolled in one."[5] Their marriage, on May 19th 1880, was very private, in the house of a Scots Presbyterian Minister, the Reverend W.A. Scott, and the two witnesses present were Dora Williams and the Minister's wife. After the service Louis

82

and Fanny took Dora Williams, an artist, to dine with them at the Viennese Bakery.

Louis was aged twenty-nine at this time, and his wife more than ten years older. On the advice of the Williamses they first went to Calistoga, a small spa-township situated to the north of San Francisco in the beautiful wine-growing district of the Napa Valley where they acquainted themselves with the Schramsberg vineyards and cellars.

In 1880 Californian wine was still experimental. Stevenson became acquainted with Jacob Schramm (later Schram), an early Californian wine grower. Schramm had begun his career as an itinerant barber. He had a shrewd business sense, and soon realized that London was a profitable market for his wines.

Louis and Fanny spent two nights in a cottage in the grounds of the Hot Springs Hotel and Lloyd Osbourne, Fanny's young son, accompanied them. Despite Thomas Stevenson's generosity, Louis had little money, and their honeymoon was passed in a deserted cottage - it was really a shack - the site of an abandoned gold and silver mine set on the Mount of St. Helena high above the Napa Valley. This rough, primitive sort of life, full of hardship and misadventures, was always congenial to Louis, and Fanny was a perfect companion, showing her practicality in buckling down to fitting calico curtains into the broken window-frames, organizing the supply of water from a well, in cooking and, above all, caring for Louis. In *Travels With a Donkey* he had once mentioned that his ideal was to camp out of doors with the woman he loved. He lacked a companion then, but now he had one.

Louis described Calistoga and its neighbourhood "a land of stage-drivers and highwaymen". It is recorded that he used the telephone for the first time there, and disliked it. Mount Saint Helena, in which he related their adventures and misadventures during their strange honeymoon, is a small township nearby. He dedicated *The Silverado Squatters* to Virgil Williams and Dora Norton Williams, and it was later finished when he made a prolonged stay in Davos, Switzerland, to be first published in *The Century Illustrated Magazine* (1883).

The two months in Silverado were on the whole happy, but they were certainly not free from trouble, for both Fanny and

Lloyd caught diphtheria, and for about forty-eight hours his wife was ill. Earlier she had smashed her thumb while carpentering, though Nellie Sanchez is curiously silent about her sister's illnesses. To Mrs. Sitwell he wrote, "My dear, we have had a miserable time. I am homesick for Europe, yet it is now a question if I shall be strong enough, for the journey home this summer."

Holding bitter memories of long days as an invalid in childhood and manhood confined to his bed, Stevenson had a special love of open air life. He wrote in *The Silverado Squatters*:

> It is one of the simple pleasures that we lose by living cribbed and covered in a house, that, though the coming of the day is still the most inspiriting, yet day's departure, also, and the return of night refresh, renew, and quiet us; and in the pastures of the dusk we stand, like cattle, exulting in the absence of the load ...

Stevenson, although he foresaw the evils of commercialization, was spared its corrupting influence, but it had already begun to invade the last decade of the nineteenth century.

A welcome visitor at Silverado on Mount St Helena was his stepson-in-law, the artist Joe Strong[6], now married to Belle, a good-natured comrade and "a capital hand at an omelette". Fittingly enough there are Samoan scenes and landscapes of Monterey at the Silverado Museum, one of the best in the world. There is a painting of the bridge at Grez-sur-Loing by Fanny and various manuscripts and first editions of R.L.S. and many other things. Among them a very pretty portrait of Louis's mother when young.

Although Fanny was well aware that Louis's parents had grave reservations about her marriage to their son, she wrote with remarkable tact and cleverness to her mother-in-law, striking just the right note. She described Louis as "my dear boy". She had had a sad time caring for him while he was ill, but she realized that it had been worse for his parents. She wrote with candour that she believed in San Francisco, Louis's soul had been purified "by the atmosphere of the Valley of the Shadow". In Scotland, Margaret Stevenson told a friend that she hoped to feel always now that Lou is being well cared for.

84

It is evident that Louis was homesick during those happy weeks as a Silverado squatter, longing for Scotland, the land of his birth. In a passage about the Scot Abroad, he wrote that there were no stars so lovely as Edinburgh street-lamps. A trifle arrogantly he continued:

> The happiest lot on earth is to be born a Scotsman....
> You have to learn the paraphrases and the Shorter Cate-
> chism; you generally take to drink; your youth, as far as
> I can find out, is a time of louder war against society, of
> more outcry and tears and turmoil, than if you had been
> born, for instance, in England. But somehow life is war-
> mer and closer; the hearth burns more redly; the lights
> of home shine softer on the rainy street....

He thought that the races which wander widest, the Jews and the Scots, were the most clannish in the world.

How often Louis and Fanny discussed their homecoming to Europe when he felt strong enough to travel, but it was not until the end of July 1880 that husband and wife, together with Lloyd Osbourne, left the Napa Valley. Louis would never return to California again, although he now loved America, but he would later travel to Saranac Lake in the Adirondacks and other parts of that great land, providing powerful stimulation for his work. On August 6th Louis and Fanny spent all day in New York looking for Will Low and his wife, only to find they were at Nantucket. The next day, together with his stepson Lloyd, they sailed from New York to Liverpool, travelling comfortable first class on *The City of Chester*. Curiously enough the day chosen was the anniversary of the day Louis had sailed in the *Devonia* for New York. When they reached Liverpool on August 17th, his parents and Sidney Colvin were there to give him and his wife the warmest of welcomes.

IX

In the Highlands' and Switzerland

At first Colvin, delighted to see Louis again and thinking that "he was looking better than I expected", was unfavourably impressed by Fanny. He told Henley that Margaret Stevenson "looked the fresher of the two", and pondered

> whether you and I will ever get reconciled to the little determined brown face and white teeth and grizzling hair, which we are to see beside him in the future.

On further acquaintance, however, Colvin was able to gauge her real character and to form an entirely different impression. He rejoiced to recognize in Stevenson's wife,

> A character as strong, as interesting, and romantic as his own, an inseparable sharer of all his thoughts, and staunch companion of all his adventures; the most open-hearted of friends to all who loved him, the most shrewd and stimulating critic of his work; and in sickness ... the most devoted and efficient of nurses.

Fanny had known little security in her life, and on entering the portals of 17 Heriot Row she was enormously impressed by the Victorian opulence of an upper-middle-class home. Her visit was a huge success. She set out to captivate her father-in-law, and the old gentleman seems to have found her not only charming, tactful, intelligent and amusing, but sharing many of the same opinions as himself. Louis really owed his reconciliation with his parents to some extent to Fanny. Thomas Stevenson with his pawky sense of humour and chivalrous sentiments towards women, took

Louis with his mother : a photograph taken in 1854.

A favourite district of Edinburgh in R.L.S.'s boyhood.

Alison Cunningham (Cummy) in old age. R.L.S.'s nanny.

Swanston Cottage, a favourite house of R.L.S.

Portrait of Robert Louis Stevenson (1890s).

Fanny Osbourne; a photograph taken about the time (1876) when she first met R.L.S.

Robert Louis Stevenson and Fanny Stevenson with Lloyd Osbourne on the veranda of Baker's Cottage at Saranac Lake in the Adirondack mountains, Upper New York State.

The 'Casco' in which Louis and his family first sailed to the South Seas.

Lloyd Osbourne, Fanny and Robert Louis Stevenson, King Kalakaua and Louis's mother Mrs. Thomas Stevenson in the cabin of the 'Casco'.

Mrs. Robert Louis Stevenson.

Robert Louis Stevenson with his man servant.

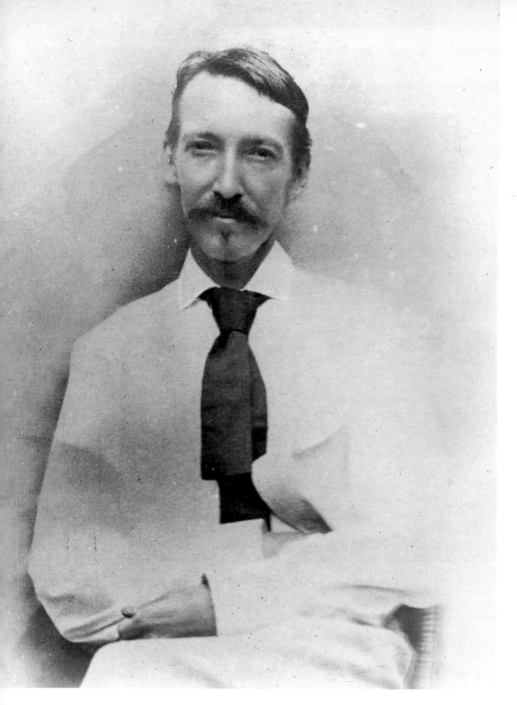

The last portrait photograph of Robert Louis Stevenson.

an immediate liking to Fanny, and delighted in her company. "I doot ye're a besom" he would say to her. The meaning of the Scottish word "besom" is a brook, and applied to a woman it means that she is a little tart in temper. Fanny, soon called him "Uncle Tom". Margaret Stevenson, secretly amused to see how well her daughter-in-law got on with her husband, also succumbed to her charm and strong character, realizing that Fanny was devoted to her son, and pleased when she declared that both his wife and mother were partners in their dedicated love to him.

Although she was absolutely dissimilar in character to her mother-in-law, describing Margaret Stevenson as "a much more complex character than her husband", Fanny became very attached to her. She usually called her "Aunt Maggie" and her father-in-law nicknamed her Cassandra, because of her pessimism. Louis and his mother were usually optimists.

In one respect Thomas Stevenson may have erred in retaining too deep a respect for Fanny's literary judgement. Although on the whole Fanny's advice to Louis on literary matters was beneficial, she was far from infallible. To make Louis promise "never to publish anything without her approval" did him no real service. An artist wants freedom to express himself. Thomas Stevenson's relations with Louis were now very affectionate. The quarrels between father and son did not occur again, nor did the bitter wrangling over religion. Only in his writings did the sharp memory of those distant times influence his work. The old, riotous Stevenson, so loved by Henley, might be partly tamed, but the rebel was never far from the surface.

One thing must have deeply saddened Louis. He would no longer be able to go to Swanston, for his father had given up Swanston Cottage earlier that summer (1880). The Stevensons did not remain long at 17 Heriot Row. It was considered that highland air would be more beneficial for Louis's health than a longer stay in Edinburgh. So the whole family, including Lloyd Osbourne, moved firstly to Blair Atholl in Perthshire and then to the Ben Wyvis Hotel in Strathpeffer, Ross. Although Louis found the scenery surrounding Strathpeffer enchanting, he disliked the Ben Wyvis Hotel intensely, sending some doggerel verses to Charles Baxter, 'On Some Ghastly Comparisons at a Spa', mocking its inmates.

To Colvin he wrote, enraptured,

> Near here is a valley, both woods, heather and a stream;
> I have laid down and died; no country, no place, was
> ever for a moment so delightful to my soul. And I have
> been a Scotsman all my life, and denied my native land!
> Away with your garden of roses, indeed! Give me the
> cool breath of Rogie Waterfall; henceforth the world for
> ever without end.

To love his native land passionately and know that his wretched
health could never stand its harsh climate! That was Louis's tragedy.
Not only was he afflicted with lung trouble, and acute chronic catarrh, but he was also consumptive. When consulted, both his uncle
Dr. George Balfour and Sir Andrew Clark said he must go to Davos
in the Swiss Alps in the winter.

Meanwhile in Strathpeffer, Thomas Stevenson, always dis-
approving of *The Amateur Emigrant* and thinking that it might in-
jure his son's reputation, had stopped its publication, for the work
was now in the hands of the publisher and Louis had been paid. His
father now reimbursed the publisher. At least Louis had the satisfaction of knowing that his story, 'The Pavilion on the Links', would
appear in *The Cornhill* in September and 'The Old Pacific Capital'
was to be published in *Fraser's* in November. At this period Stevenson contemplated a history of Scotland and its clans to please his
father, but this project eventually came to nothing.

Louis was now aged almost thirty. Before leaving for Switzerland, he was eager to pass two weeks in London, and to see some
of his friends, Colvin, Gosse, Lang and Henley, not least to visit
the Savile Club. Fanny sensed that they would regard her with mis-
giving, very uneasy that their relations with Louis would be affected
by his marriage. Above all, she was determined to guard Louis's
health, and she was aware that the long hours of bibulous talk with
his friends was harmful to him. It was now that the antagonism
between Henley and Fanny smouldered, for Henley loved Louis,
and feared that Fanny's influence would come between him and
his friend. He ought to have been more understanding, for he was
devoted to his own wife, Anna.* Perhaps Fanny was too possess-

* Louis, when corresponding with Henley, usually refers to Anna as
"the Chatelaine".

ive and jealous of the friends he had known in his bachelor days, but she thought Henley far too boisterous. She knew Louis lived for his writing, and was sorely afraid that his frail health would not stand the late hours and the over-excitement. She complained to her mother-in-law in Edinburgh that London was a most unhealthful place at this season (autumn 1880).

> It is not good for my mind, nor my body either, to sit smiling at Louis's friends, until I feel like a hypocritical Cheshire cat ... and all the time furtively watching the clock and thirsting for their blood because they stay so late.[1]

Gosse, though he later had friction with Fanny at Braemar, was intrigued by her unusual character and later wrote of her:

> She was one of the strangest people who have lived in our time, a sort of savage nature in some ways, but very lovable - extraordinarily passionate and unlike everybody else in her violent feelings and unrestrained ways of expressing things picturesquely, but not literary. I think R.L.S. must have caught some of his ways of feeling from her.

Both Louis and Fanny were careless regarding their financial affairs, and while staying at the Grosvenor Hotel were too extravagant in entertaining Louis's friends. He was obliged to appeal to his parents.

At the end of October, Louis, Fanny and Lloyd, together with their black thoroughbred Skye terrier, a gift of Sir Walter Simpson (Stevenson's companion on the *Inland Voyage*) began their arduous journey to Switzerland.[2] The dog was usually called Wattie, Woggie or Woggin or Woggs. In 1880, Davos, their destination, was inaccessible by train, and to reach it they had to travel by sleigh for eight hours after the slow journey through France. During their first visit to Davos, the Stevensons stayed in the Belvedere Hotel, a small establishment then, but much enlarged later on. Davos is about 5,000 feet above sea-level, and surrounded by pine woods, and is for five months of the year under snow. Louis felt depressed and ill, sensing that a "Swiss mountain valley had a certain prison-like effect on the imagination".

Among the books he had brought with him to Davos, was Hawley's *Operations of War*, a present from an old general, a friend of Thomas Stevenson. Louis, throughout his life, was always fascinated by the scientific study of the art of war. It was a strange taste for a born writer, but compelled at various periods to inaction and the life of an invalid by his ill health, he occasionally gave way to frustration. He wrote his father: "I am drowned in it (the book) a thousand fathoms deep; and O that I had been a soldier, is still my cry!" Perhaps Stevenson had some distant memory of a former existence as a soldier. It was now that a close friendship was forged between Louis and his stepson Lloyd, for nothing pleased him more than to play with toy soldiers, planning campaigns in a chilly Davos attic.

Though he disliked most of the English residents in the hotel, Stevenson carried a letter of introduction from Edmund Gosse to John Addington Symonds, the distinguished art historian, a fellow invalid and author of the seven-volume *History of the Italian Renaissance*. His friendship with Symonds was a consolation for his enforced stay of six months in Davos, and he became a favourite companion on his walks. Louis also much liked and admired his doctor, Dr. Ruedi, a tall and genial man, son of Dr. Luzius Ruedi, the original discoverer of the beneficial and healing qualities of the Alpine climate.[3] Fanny, too, consulted Dr. Ruedi for she often felt far from well in Davos as she disliked heights. She was afraid of becoming too stout, and the doctor told her that it was owing to a disease of the stomach and he put her on a diet.

Louis was not yet famous when he first came to Davos, but he was becoming well known as the author of *An Inland Voyage* and *Travels With a Donkey*. He wrote several essays, including one on 'Samuel Pepys'[4] for *The Cornhill*. In the preface to the work, he felt that he had been amply just to his memory. The passage about respectability seems autobiographical and to have significance.

> When writers inveigle against respectability, in the present degraded meaning of the word, they are suspected of a taste for clay pipes and beer cellars, and their per-

formances are thought to hail from the *owl's nest* of the comedy.... For to do anything because others do it, and not because the thing is good, or kind, or honest in its own right, is to resign all moral control upon yourself, and go post-haste to the devil with the greater number.

He also wrote four descriptive essays about Davos, printed later in the *Pall Mall Gazette* in February and March, 1881, as 'Essays on Travel'. He toyed with the idea of writing a life of the Duke of Wellington who had died in 1852, but nothing came of it. Far from idle while in very indifferent health in Switzerland, he was busy preparing for the press his collected essays, *Virginibus Puerisque* (published April 1881).

In his essays *Virginibus Puerisque*, Louis airs his views about marriage, but it was written in 1876 several years before his marriage to Fanny. It is original and rather cynical in tone. "Marriage is terrifying," he wrote, "but so is a cold and forlorn old age."

> The friendships of men are vastly agreeable, but they are insecure... Marriage is certainly a perilous remedy. Instead of one, two or three, you stake your happiness on one life only.

It is evident that Stevenson, extremely well-read, was familiar with Bacon's essay of 'Marriage and Single Life', "He that hath wife and children, hath given Hostages to Fortune; for they are impediments, to Great Enterprise, either of Vertue, or Mischiefe."[5]

In his lively way Stevenson sees its disadvantages:

> But marriage, if comfortable, is not at all heroic. It certainly narrows and damps the spirits of generous men. In marriage, a man becomes slack and selfish, and undergoes a fatty degeneration of his moral being.

At twenty-six Stevenson was writing for his own age group, who shared the same problems of inexperience. He dedicated *Virginibus Puerisque* to William Ernest Henley, who wanted at this period to marry an Edinburgh girl, Anna Boyle, as soon as he had acquired sufficient financial security. Of his other friends, Colvin was to wait until 1903 before marrying Frances Sitwell, Baxter was to wed in 1877, and Simpson in 1874.

Christmas 1880 was a happy time for Louis, for he could indulge in two of his favourite diversions, tobogganing and skating. He wrote to his mother on December 26th,

> I was very tired yesterday and could not write, tobogganed so furiously all morning; we had a delightful day, crowned by an incredible dinner - more courses than I have fingers on my hands.[6]

A very welcome visitor to Davos was Frances Sitwell, so much loved by Louis during his impressionable years in Edinburgh and France. She was desperately worried about her surviving son Bertie, now eighteen, who was ill from a lung disease and succumbed to it in April 1881. To comfort his dear friend, Louis wrote his lovely verses 'In Memorial F.A.S.', now included in *Underwoods*.[7] Here are two verses:

> Yet, O stricken heart, remember, O remember
> How of human days he lived the better part.
> April came to bloom and never dim December
> Breathed its killing chills upon the head or heart.
>
> Doomed to know not winter, only spring, a being
> Trod the flowery April blithely for a while,
> Took his fill of music, joy of thought and seeing,
> Came and stayed and went, nor ever ceased to smile.

At Davos, Stevenson began a warm friendship with Horatio F. Brown, an author intimate with John Addington Symonds, and when he returned to Venice sent him a copy of William Penn's *Fruits of Solitude*, a book printed in Philadelphia and one dear to Louis, for he had carried it in his pocket all over San Francisco.

When Colvin arrived in Davos during January, he found Louis very tired of Switzerland and very depressed. In the spring he wrote him that he had never remained so long in one place as Davos. "That tells of my old gipsy nature; like a violin hung up, I begin to lose what music there was in me."

Lloyd was now in a boarding-school in England, and at the end of April, Louis left Davos to rejoin his wife in Paris. After a stay at Barbizon to visit his old haunts, they moved to Paris where Louis wrote his parents, "A week in Paris reduced me to the limpness and lack of appetite peculiar to a kid glove, and gave Fanny a jumping, sore throat." At St. Germain-en-Laye they pitched on the Star and Garter (they call it somebody's pavilion)[8] and it was here that Louis heard the nightingale for the first time in his life, and found the place a bed of lilacs at the beginning of May.

Now came a very creative period for Louis. Almost the whole of June and July 1881 he and Fanny were at Pitlochry, Perthshire, staying in Kinnaird Cottage above that town, near Moulin, with a view of the purple moorlands reaching to Ben Vrackie, and the gentle murmur of a burn nearby, "a lovely spot, a sweet spot with its little green glen".

Fanny had a taste for the supernatural - she was certainly psychic - and may well have encouraged Louis to work on a series of stories of terror, or "crawlers" as he called them. The eerie and the ghastly always fascinated him.

Stimulated by his return to his beloved Scotland, Stevenson wrote one of his best works of fiction, his story *Thrawn Janet*. His masterly characterization of the austere Scottish minister, the Reverend Murdoch Soulis, cannot be perfected, and no work reveals more clearly his preoccupation with evil and the devil, characteristic of Scottish Calvinism.

Louis was elated by *Thrawn Janet* "but it frightened me to death" he wrote to Colvin. Louis, usually so critical of his own work, never doubted that *Thrawn Janet* was good. He sent it to Leslie Stephen, fearing that he would not accept it as it was in Scottish dialect, but Stephen published it in *The Cornhill* during October. The Anglo-Saxon reader may be deterred from reading it because of the dialect, but Henry James, who first became acquainted with Stevenson during his sojourn later in Bournemouth, was warm in his praise, calling it "a masterpiece" and among his shorter stories "the strongest in execution".

Stevenson's next work *The Body-Snatcher*, a gruesome tale, was "laid aside, in a justifiable disgust, the tale being horrid."[9] However, it was published three years later in the *Pall Mall Gazette*.

Louis, whilst in Pitlochry, began a powerful story of the sea, named *The Merry Men*, which he called "a fantastic sonata about the sea and wrecks." "I like it much above all my other attempts at story-telling," he told Colvin. Fanny, too, was trying her hand at writing, working on *The Shadow on the Bed*.

Stevenson much valued the criticism of Henley when he sent him a draft of *The Merry Men*, though he sometimes carped at it.

The Merry Men derives its curious name from the giant breakers off the south-west coast of Aros. "And it's here," wrote Stevenson,

> that these big breakers dance together - the dance of death, it may be called. I have heard it said that they run fifty feet high; but that must be the green water only, for the spray runs twice as high as that. Whether they got their name from their movements, which are swift and antic, or from the "shouting" they make about the turning of the tide, so that all Aros shakes with it, is more than I can tell.[10]

What an extraordinary affinity Stevenson had with the sea! Stevenson is again preoccupied with evil, the greed in the mind of the narrator's uncle, Gordon Darnaway, leading him slowly and inexorably, as if by divine justice, to be drowned at the scene of his crime. When writing *The Merry Men* Stevenson made use of his vivid memories as a young man of his visit to Erraid, off Mull. Mrs. Sim, their landlady at Pitlochry, who owned Kinnaird Cottage, was a Highland woman, strongly psychic as many Highlanders are. She was fond of relating ghost stories to Louis and Fanny and they would listen, entranced at her eerie tales. The weather, that summer in Scotland, was extremely wet and stormy, and Louis was much confined to the sitting-room, where he worked on his fiction. When possible, Louis would walk to a little glen with a burn nearby, "a wonderful burn" he told Colvin, gold and green and snow-white, singing loud and low in different steps of its career, now pouring over miniature crags, now fretting itself to death in a maze of rock stairs and pots.[11]

Stevenson never liked to be far from water.

When Professor Aeneas Mackay retired from the Chair of Constitutional Law and History at Edinburgh University, Louis, wanting a more solid income than he acquired by his writings, decided to apply for the vacancy, and he succeeded in obtaining many testimonials from his friends. However, his academic qualifications were not sufficient, and he failed to get it.

At the beginning of August, Louis and Fanny moved from Pitlochry to Braemar, where they stayed at "the late Miss M'Gregor's cottage", though Louis told his friends his correct address was The Cottage, Castleton of Braemar. There is a plaque to denote the cottage.

Here, Fanny liked to watch Queen Victoria drive in her open carriage, showing "a true Scotch spirit in her indifference to the weather". She was on the way to Balmoral.[12] However, she tempered her enthusiasm for "the sturdy old lady" with sympathy, for her two ladies-in-waiting, looking unhappy and cross as they sat back to the horses.

Poor Louis nursed a horrible cold as he wrote to Frances Sitwell in August. Although the country at Braemar was beautiful, the weather was even worse than at Pitlochry. "The wind pipes, the rain comes in squalls, great black clouds are continually overhead, and it is as cold as March." It was here at Braemar in his native Scotland that Stevenson began the book, firstly named *The Sea-Cook*, which would make him famous.

In 'The Art of Writing'[13] Louis relates,

On a chill September morning, by the cheek of a brisk fire, and the rain drumming on the window, I began *The Sea-Cook*, for that was the original title.

Louis's original inspiration was certainly a map. He says that his imagination was first ignited by a flat piece of paper on which an amateur map had been painted by himself.

> On one of these occasions I made the map of an island; it was elaborately and (I thought) beautifully coloured: the shape of it took my fancy beyond expression; it contained harbours that pleased me like sonnets; as I pored over my map of Treasure Island the future character of the book began to appear there visibly among imaginary woods; and their brown faces and light weapons peeped out upon me from unexpected quarters, and as they passed to and fro, fighting and hunting treasure.

Louis often remained a boy at heart, taking a childish delight in simple pleasures. His stepson Lloyd's enthusiasm and joy when Louis showed him the map, must also have inspired him to write the book.

It is curious that Fanny, sometimes a good critic of her husband's work, at first disparaged *Treasure Island*, writing later from Davos to Edmund Gosse's wife,

> I am glad Mr. Gosse liked "Treasure Island" (in *Young Folks*). I don't. I liked the beginning but after that the life seemed to go out of it, and it became tedious.[14]

In this she reveals poor literary judgement because the work, as it develops, is very dramatic, while Louis's plays intended for the theatre lack drama. Later Fanny, as the widow of a famous writer, could conveniently remember the occasions when Louis would read portions of his work to his entranced listeners, his voice altogether thrilling, sympathetic and dramatic. Both Colvin and Gosse - visitors to Braemar - and appreciative listeners to *The Sea-Cook* - encouraged Louis to write his novel, over the years as much loved by adults as juveniles.

Among Louis's visitors to the cottage at Braemar were his father and mother, 'Auntie' and Dr. Alexander Japp, who had corresponded with Stevenson about Thoreau. Japp could not have been more helpful, for having heard the author reciting *Treasure Island* and knowing a proprietor named Henderson of the popular boys' magazine *Young Folks*, he arranged for it to be serialized as *Treasure Island*, by "Captain George North". It appeared as such between October 1881 and January 1882, but never enjoyed popularity in serial form as it did later as a book.

The most enthisiastic of Louis's listeners, to the early chapters, was his own father. Louis relates:[15]

> My father caught fire at once with all the romance and childishness of his original nature. His own stories, that every night of his life he put himself to sleep with, dealt perpetually with ships, roadside inns, robbers, old sailors and commercial travellers before the era of steam. But in *Treasure Island* he recognized something kindred to his own imagination, it was *his* kind of picturesque; and he not only heard with delight the daily chapter, but set himself acting to collaborate.

Those days, of late summer when rain lashed against the window panes, would linger long in the memory of Edmund Gosse. What an achievement for Louis, struggling with ill-health and plagued by his cough, forbidden to speak, and lying in bed, to read passages of his work, with his gesticulating finger and with his powerful, dramatic voice. Sometimes he played a silent game of chess with Gosse.

There is an interesting letter to Henley in August 25th, 1881 where he discusses his "crawlers":

> I am now on another lay for the moment, purely owing to Lloyd, this one, but I believe there's more coin in it than in any amount of "crawlers": now, see here, *The Sea-Cook* or *Treasure Island*: a story for Boys.
>
> If this don't fetch the kids, why, they have gone rotten since my day. Will you be surprised to learn that it is about Buccaneers, that it begins in The Admiral Benbow public-house on the Devon coast, that it's all about a map and a treasure, and a mutiny and a derelict ship, and a current, and a fine old Squire Trelawney (the real

Tre, purged of literature and sin, to suit the infant mind) and a doctor, and another doctor, and a sea-cook with one leg, and a sea-song with the chorus "Yo-ho-ho and a bottle of rum".

Louis tells Henley that Lloyd had ordered no women in the story. Actually there is one, minor character, the mother of the narrator Jim Hawkins. "Long John Silver", one of Stevenson's most successful creations, was modelled on the character of W.E. Henley. To his friend he later wrote: "It was the sight of your maimed strength and masterfulness that begot John Silver." The letter was written at Hyères in May 1883.

The most convincing characters are those dabbling in evil and violence, such as the Coxswain Israel Hands. *Treasure Island* was published in 1883 and by 1895, a year after his death, had made him £75,000.

During the early autumn, Louis was again smitten with throat and lung troubles and was ordered by his doctors to return to Davos in October. This time he and Fanny and Lloyd occupied a small house all to themselves, the Châlet au Stein, near the Buol Hotel. Whilst in London Henley had introduced him to the publishing house of Chatto and Windus, which agreed to republish his biographical essays as *Familiar Studies of Men and Books* and two volumes of *New Arabian Nights*. Henley sometimes acted as an unpaid literary agent to Stevenson until 1885. In Switzerland, Stevenson again enjoyed the companionship of John Addington Symonds, but during November Symonds found him

> lying, ghastly in bed - purple cheek-bones, yellow cheeks, bloodless eyes - fever all over him - without appetite - and all about him so utterly forlorn, with the black Scotch terrier Woggs "squealing", and Fanny nursing him.[16]

Then Fanny fell seriously ill with a liver complaint, drain-poisoning and diarrhoea. Accompanied by Lloyd as sick-nurse, she was forced to leave for Berne for further treatment. So, Stevenson was left alone with a Swiss-German cook, who was somewhat incompetent, though she no doubt found him a difficult invalid.

Stevenson now felt homesick for Edinburgh and wrote to Charles Baxter:

> Pray write me something cheery: a little Edinburgh gossip, in Heaven's name. Ah! What I would not give you to steal this evening with you through the big, echoing, college archway, and away south under the street lamps, and away to dear Brash's, now defunct!

Dear memories came back to him, the night at Bonny mainhead, the Compass near the sign of the *Twinkling Eye*, and one haunting memory when he lay on the pavement in misery.[17]

Despite his wretched health, Louis managed to finish *Treasure Island*. He was hard at work also on *The Silverado Squatters* and various essays, including the first 'Talk and Talkers', and a new novel *Prince Otto*. Louis missed Fanny's and Lloyd's companionship, and he went to meet them in Berne. On December 26th, 1881, writing to his mother of an adventurous journey "in an open sleigh - seven hours on end - through whole forests of Christmas trees". The cold was beyond belief. Fanny and Lloyd were wretched, but Louis sang in an imitation of a street singer, and Lloyd remarked, "You seem to be the only one with any courage left." Louis by this time was heartily tired of Davos.

During February 1882, Louis wrote to his old nurse Alison Cunningham, for she had been unwell for a long time. He told her about his domestic life, how "a fine, canny, twinkling, shrewd, auld-fauant peasant body" and a good cook had succeeded their pretty, but incompetent maid. "God bless you, my dear 'Cummy'," Stevenson ended his letter.

Whilst in Switzerland Stevenson continued to "bury Henley in copy" as if he was his private secretary. In a letter written from the Châlet au Stein during April 1882, he refers to £100 received from Henley. Whether it was a loan or not is far from clear. In this letter he refers to Byron:

> Byron not only wrote *Don Juan*, he called Joan of Arc "a fanatical strumpet". These are his words. I think the double shame, first to a great poet, second to an English noble, passes words.

In his love for France, Stevenson would not lightly forgive Byron for this phrase.

In his work *The Influence of Books*, Stevenson relates

> that everybody has been influenced by Wordsworth ...
> a certain innocence, a rugged austerity of joy, a sight of
> the stars, the silence that is in the lonely hills, some-
> thing of the cold thrill of dawn, cling to his work.

It is evident that Stevenson was very familiar with the poet. In a letter to Baxter written in early 1879, Stevenson wrote:

> There are no manners and customs, but men and women
> grow up like trees in a still, well-walled garden at their
> own sweet will.

This is reminiscent of Wordsworth's famous poem composed upon Westminster Bridge (September 3rd, 1801). In a further letter to Baxter from Heriot Row, Stevenson quotes the lines from "Intimations of Immortality" from *Recollections of Early Childhood*:

> Though nothing can bring back the hour
> Of splendour in the grass, of glory in the flower.

Indeed Stevenson, so widely read, was influenced by Shakespeare, especially by *Hamlet* and Kent's speech, so overpowering when King Lear was dying. *The Pilgrim's Progress*, "a book that breathes of every beautiful and valuable emotion", was one of his favourites. Dumas, particularly *The Vicomte de Braglelonne*, with its chivalrous d'Artagnan, was loved by him in his youth, as were *The Meditations of Marcus Aurelius* appealing to the mature man.

Goethe's Biography by Lewes, he admits had a profound influence on him, though he knew nobody he less admired. He wrote with insight. Biography, usually so false to its office, does here, for once, perform for us some of the work of fiction, reminding us, that is, of the true tissue of man's nature, and how huge faults and virtues cohabit and persevere in the same character.

X

The Restless Years

In the spring of 1882, Louis's much esteemed Dr. Ruedi said that his patient was well enough to leave Davos, but suggested that he and Fanny should now live in the South of France. However, Stevenson left Davos in April and instead of going at once to France, where their doctor had sanctioned them to live "fifteen miles as the crow flies from the sea, and if possible near a fir wood"[1], they went firstly to London and Edinburgh. Presumably craving Louis's and Fanny's company, his parents suggested that they should all share a rented house named Stobo Manse, near Peebles. There during July they stayed for two weeks, but it rained every day, "and it is low, damp and *mauchy*" complained Louis to Henley in a letter. It was characteristic of Stevenson to invent fictional characters when writing to his friends and old Pegfurth Bannatyne and Pirbright Smith with their recollections of Hazlitt and Wordsworth, were both creatures of his imagination.

The stay at Stobo Manse was harmful to Louis's health, and he was compelled to leave for London, where he consulted Sir Andrew Clarke. Whilst there, Stevenson began his short story *The Treasure of Franchard*, set in the country surrounding Fontainebleau. With his memories of Grez, he makes Dr. Duprez say to his adopted son Jean-Marie: "I have always had a fancy to be a fish in summer, Jean-Marie, here in the Loing beside Grez." There were memories of beautiful June days when Louis sat upon the hill above the village, "it seemed as if every blade of grass must hide a cigale," he wrote, and the fields rang merrily with their music, jingling far and near as with the sleigh bells of the fairy Queen.[2]

Andrew Clarke recommended Speyside and accompanied by Sidney Colvin, to be later joined by the Stevenson family, Louis passed a month at Kingussie in Invernessshire, where he continued to write *Treasure of Franchard*. Despite the beauty of the purple hills, the music of its silvery river Spey and a few glorious days in September, Kingussie did not suit Louis's health. He suffered another haemorrhage. Kingussie was to be his last view of Scotland. Returning to London, Andrew Clarke stressed that it was essential for him to go to a warmer climate.

Then followed a vain quest for a climate not only beneficial to Louis's health, but an atmosphere congenial for his work. Nellie Sanchez, in her life of her sister, wrote that Fanny was too ill to travel during September 1882 to Marseilles, but Louis, accompanied by his cousin Bob, started for that town in the middle of the month. At Montpellier, Louis was seized with another bad attack of haemorrhage, and Fanny, extremely anxious, though very unwell, hurried to Marseilles to meet him, for Bob had been obliged to return home. They signed a lease for a house, the Campagne Defli, near S. Marcel, a suburb of Marseilles.

It was in a lovely spot, Fanny wrote, so like Indiana "that it would not surprise me to hear my father or mother speak to me at any moment".[3] They intended it to be their permanent home, but the place did not suit Louis's health and he again succumbed to haemorrhage and attack of fever. For Fanny it was a nightmare. For two whole days Louis lay insensible as if dead. It may well be that the house was in an unhealthy situation, since Louis had written to Bob before moving in: "The Campagne Demosquito goes on nightly, and is very deadly. Ere we can get installed, we shall be beggared to the door, I see."[4] When an epidemic of fever broke out in St. Marcel in December, Fanny, much agitated, arranged for Louis to go to Nice. Her problems were aggravated by linguistic difficulties, for she hardly spoke French at all, making her impatient with servants, even if they were good cooks. To wriggle out of the lease presented a problem, but they succeeded in doing so, during February 1883.

Before moving into their new home, the Châlet la Solitude at Hyères, a tiny Swiss chalet with elegant Swiss gables and balcony, just outside the *vieille ville*, it was already February. Louis wrote again to "Cummy" from Nice, telling her that she must think him one of the meanest rogues in creation for not writing earlier. He intends to dedicate the little verses he is writing, *A Child's Garden of Verses*, to her, for she is the only person who will really understand them. His wife had been ill, owing to overwork and anxiety about his own health. To Henley he sent many verses of *The Child's Garden*.

Stevenson was very happy in the Chậlet la Solitude at 4 rue Victor Basch, where there is a plaque:

> HERE
> DURING 1883-1884
> LIVED THE ENGLISH AUTHOR
> ROBERT LOUIS STEVENSON
> HE DECLARED 'I WAS
> ONLY HAPPY ONCE:
> THAT WAS AT
> HYERES.'[5]

He loved the tiny house and its garden with its gnarled olive trees, its nightingales and the moonlit nights, reminding him, perhaps, of Silverado. Above all, he found the atmosphere of the house congenial for his work, and it was one of those rare times when he was alone with Fanny, Lloyd being away at school.

He finished his book *Prince Otto* and started his historical novel, *The Black Arrow*, a tale set in the fifteenth century during the Wars of the Roses. Stevenson found *The Paston Letters* helpful for a background. His object was now to earn money. It is a lively, adventure story for boys of fifteen, with convincing dialogue, likely to appeal to Lloyd. Stevenson was interested in the character of the young Richard Crookback (later Richard III) and he emerges briefly towards the end of the book. Curiously enough, it was at first more successful than *Treasure Island* when serialized by James Henderson in *Young Folks*, though a much inferior work.

He still corresponded with Mrs. Sitwell, writing her from Hyères about *A Child's Garden of Verses* and mentioning *Prince Otto*, "a sore burthen, but a hopefull".[6] He is going to make a fortune, but he is not yet clear of debt. Louis always remained grateful to Frances Sitwell, for he owed to her much happiness. He knew little about gardening but he wrote sometimes to his parents, telling them that their lovely garden was invaded by snails. Not having the heart to slay them, he deposited them near a neighbour's garden wall.

To Edmund Gosse he owed part of the publication of *The Silverado Squatters* in the New York Century magazine. He tells him on May 20th that his garden is a riot of colours, of roses, of aloes, and fig-marigolds, of silvery olives, with a graceful view of the mountains.

During the middle of the Provençal summer, Stevenson joined his parents at the Baths of Royat, in Auvergne. His stay provided him with material for a recently discovered short story, *The Enchantress*. It is likely that it was written much later, on Stevenson's 1889 voyage from Hawaii to Samoa in the South Seas, on the schooner *Equator*.[7] According to Lloyd Osbourne the story "was written on a yacht when everybody had to write a yarn and read it aloud". The story is entertaining, so it is difficult to understand why Lloyd denigrated it and refused to allow it to be printed. Possibly he considered it too biographical, his mother having first met Stevenson in France. She was a very determined character, like Miss Croft in the story. Alternatively Lloyd may have thought the work uncharacteristic of his stepfather's writings.

When Louis returned to Châlet la Solitude in the late summer, he received news from Scotland, causing a desperate sadness. His dear friend of Edinburgh days, Walter Ferrier, had died. He was an alcoholic, partial to opium, and his weakness had led to a rapid decline in his fortunes. Louis writes of Ferrier, so much loved, with sensitivity and imagination. It was tragic that Walter, so gifted, yet whose life had been wasted, should have died. As he wrote to Henley on September 19th:[8]

> The curse was on him. Even his friends did not know him but by fits. I have passed hours with him when he was so wise, good and sweet, that I never knew the like of it in any other.

Perhaps in some queer way Ferrier reminded him of his much admired Edinburgh poet Robert Fergusson, for drink had hastened the early deaths of both men. It is with infinite sadness that Louis writes of Walter in his essay 'Old Mortality' (*Memories and Portraits*): "The tale of this great failure is, to those who remained true to him, the tale of a success." Perhaps Louis felt a tinge of guilt that he had once encouraged Walter in his addiction to opium, for his friend's mother had written earlier, bitterly accusing Louis of collusion in her son's downward career. Walter's sister Coggie, however, resembled him in his gentle nature, and she was later, during the summer of 1884, to visit them and become a valued friend of both Louis and Fanny. As Louis wrote to Bob, "He was, after you, the oldest of my friends."

On New Year's Day 1884, Louis was able to write to his father from 'La Solitude' that he had £50 in the bank and that his total receipts for the year were £465.0.6d. His sojourn at Hyères continued a creative period, and he wrote to Colvin in early March, "two chapters of *Otto* do remain: one to rewrite, one to create, and I am not yet able to tackle them." Fanny had gone for a drive to "certain meadows which are now one street of jonquils, seabound meadows".

Stevenson had a high opinion of Walter Scott's works. He wrote Mr. Dick, the head clerk of the family firm of Stevenson in Edinburgh that *The Waverley Novels* were better to reread than *The Life of Scott*. He told his father that he thought *Kenilworth* better than *Waverley* and *Nigel* too, and *Quentin Durward* about as good. He considered that the slap-dash and the shoddy grew upon him with success.

Only Stevenson's indomitable courage sustained him. Whilst in Nice in early January, Louis had a sudden attack of internal congestion and nearly died from it. Although he occasionally succumbed to fits of acute depression, Stevenson was an invincible optimist. The dramatic critic, his friend William Archer, later described him as "an aggressive optimist". In April 1884 he had serious eye trouble, and was too blind to read. In May, his essay 'Old Mortality' was published and he informed "Dear Boy" Henley that Coggie Ferrier, who was staying with him and Fanny at Hyères, liked it. When Miss Ferrier read aloud to them *Thrawn Janet*, Stevenson was quite bowled over by his own work.

To his mother he wrote a glowing tribute to his wife after four years of marriage:

> I love her better than ever and admire her more, and I
> cannot think what I have done to deserve so good a gift.
> ... My marriage has been the most successful in the world
> ... she is everything to me. Wife, brother, sister, daughter

and dear companion and I would not change to get a goddess or a saint.

Yet Fanny, despite her selfless nursing of her husband, was a hypochondriac, subject to morbid depression, and being much influenced by those moods could not have given him sage advice. Graham Balfour relates that on hearing the doctor's diagnosis of his eye trouble as opthalmia, Fanny "sat and gloomed in another room".[9] Lloyd relates that his mother subscribed to *The Lancet* and became over-anxious about "all sorts of bogies". She warned her husband against eating salads, for they carried the eggs of tape-worms, and salt hardened one's arteries and shortened one's days.[10] Her constant anxiety for his health gave her absurd prejudices.

Although Louis had been so happy in Hyères, an outbreak of cholera erupted in the *vielle ville* and Fanny persuaded him to leave Hyères. She could now rely on extra help when nursing Louis, for a French-Swiss girl, Valentine Roch, had recently entered the Stevenson household, to be treated as one of the family. Fanny gave her instructions what to do if her husband had a haemorrhage when she was alone with him. Whilst ill in bed, Louis had heard of Edmund Gosse's appointment as Clark Reader in English Literature at Trinity College, Cambridge. His first reaction had been one of envy.

On his return to England, Stevenson stayed for a few weeks in Richmond. Lloyd was now at school in Bournemouth. Thomas and Margaret Stevenson rejoiced that Louis and Fanny had returned to Great Britain, and in September 1884 they decided to move to Bournemouth, partly to be near Lloyd, and partly because Louis's doctor had recommended this resort because it was then renowned for its healthy air, its pine trees and heath. Another motive for living in Bournemouth for the next three years was that Thomas Stevenson's health was failing, for he had lately suffered several strokes. One wonders, however, whether Louis would have been better advised to return to Hyères once the cholera epidemic had abated. Louis and Fanny first found accommodation at Wensleydale on the West Cliff, then they stayed for a time in a furnished house in Branksome Park called Bonnalie Towers which had neither towers nor turrets. Stevenson certainly was a dual personality, and this fascinating facet of his make-up can be perceived more sharply during the Bournemouth period of his life, when he wrote *Dr. Jekyll and Mr. Hyde*. In Stevenson's double life he used to pose, as a youth, but there was an aura of sham in his play-acting, when he wandered round Edinburgh hoping to be arrested as a vagabond.

Louis's and Fanny's final home in the West Cliff, Bournemouth, for three years, was a secluded house called "Seaview", renamed "Skerryvore" after Alan Stevenson's lighthouse on Dhu Heartach. It was a long-delayed wedding present from Thomas Stevenson to Fanny, and they moved into it round about Easter 1885. Fanny became particularly fond of the house and worked hard to improve the garden, according to William Archer, the dramatic critic, who was to become a close friend of Louis's.

Writing in *The Critic* (November 5, 1885) Archer described the garden, beautifully situated at the top of Alum Chine.

> The demesne extends over the edge, and almost to the bottom of the Chine, and here, amid laurel and rhododendron, broom and gorse, the garden merges into a network of paths and stairways, with tempting seats and unexpected arbors at every turn.

Archer was impressed, as most people were by Mrs. Stevenson's unmistakable strength of character. Although of small stature, "her hair is an unglossy black, and her complexion darker than one would expect in a woman of Dutch extraction." Here, at Skerryvore, Fanny established herself as Louis's guardian, never allowing anybody ever with a cold to enter its portals. She furnished her home with taste, and having a discerning eye for colour, made it both light and pretty.

Earlier whilst lodging in Wensleydale, Stevenson collaborated with Henley in writing two plays, *Admiral Guinea* and *Beau Austin*. They wrongly supposed that they would make a lot of money from these ventures. Thomas, although his relations with his son were now extremely harmonious, protested at the representation on the stage of one of the characters named Pen in *Admiral Guinea*,[11] affirming that it was profane blackguarding. His strong religious convictions were offended, but Louis in a letter written at Bonallie Towers to soften the old man's displeasure, tried to explain his purpose in writing. Louis's dramatic sense, so powerful in his novels and short stories, seems to have waned when he wrote for the theatre. One senses a divergence of aims between Louis and Henley about this time, because the former lost his conviction that he would ever become a popular dramatist, while Henley always retained his faith in *Beau Austin* and *Deacon Brodie*. There were mutual recriminations between wife and friend. Henley always disliked Fanny's influence on Louis's work and Fanny considered, not without justification, Henley too boisterous and overpowering when collaborating with her husband at Bournemouth, thus blaming him for the deterioration in his health. Lloyd, however, who was rapidly acquiring literary aspirations, did not share his mother's growing dislike of Henley. He had a terrific admiration for the exuberant, red-bearded writer, with his loud laugh, dependent on a crutch. "Never was there such another as William Ernest Henley," he wrote; "he had an unimaginable fire and vitality; he swept one off one's feet." When he read aloud *Beau Austin* set in Tunbridge Wells in 1820, he did so, so movingly and tenderly that Lloyd's eyes were wet with tears.

Fanny had no great talent either for writing or for painting. While Louis was ill in bed at Hyères she conceived the ideas for some short stories about dynamite. She collaborated with Louis in a novel named *The Dynamiter*, but Louis was almost certainly the real author of the work. Fanny, always sensitive, felt humiliated that she had been given insufficient credit for her part in the novel. It was published in April 1886 by Longmans as *More Arabian Nights* when the Stevensons had already moved to Bournemouth.

Bournemouth: A Creative Period

In his early life, Stevenson had clearly possessed socialist inclinations - young men often do - but later in his career he became almost an imperialist with a great pride of country. Like Queen Victoria, and many of his contemporaries, Stevenson bitterly blamed William Gladstone, the Prime Minister, for his delay in sending an expedition to save the life of Gordon of Khartoum, murdered by the Mahdi's forces in 1885. He wrote more understandingly from Bonallie Towers, Bournemouth, during February to Sidney Colvin:

> O dear! in this prolical scene of degradation, much must be forgiven. I fear England is dead of Burgessy, and only walks about galvanised. I do not love to think of my countrymen these days, nor to remember myself. Why was I silent? I feel I have no right to blame any one but I won't write to the G.O.M.

To his friend J.A. Symonds, a permanent invalid in Davos, he wrote:

> Millais (I hear) was painting Gladstone when the news came of Gordon's death; Millais was much affected, and Gladstone said, "Why? *It is the man's own temerity!* Voila le Bourgeois! Le voila nu! But why should I blame Gladstone, when I too am a Bourgeois? When I have held my peace?

When somebody told Stevenson that Gladstone had sat up "till two in the morning to finish *Treasure Island*",[1] he contemptuously remarked that "he would do better to attend to the imperial affairs of England." Today venerated as one of our greatest statesmen, Gladstone seemed to Stevenson a symbol of the bourgeois respectability he rejected.

Louis and Fanny made many new friends while living at Skerryvore, but their most important friendship developed during the autumn of 1884 with Henry James, Fanny's fellow-countryman, best known as the author of *The American, The Portrait of a Lady, Daisy Miller* and *Roderick Hudson*. Neither Stevenson nor James took to one another when they first became acquainted during the summer of 1879, before Louis's journey to California. James called Louis "a pleasant feller, but a shirt-collarless bohemian" and a great deal (in an inoffensive way) of a poseur. He considered, however, his *Inland Voyage* a charming work.

An intimate friendship ripened between the two writers after the publication of Henry James's essay 'The Art of Fiction' in *Longman's Magazine* (September 1884), an answer to a published lecture by a contemporary novelist Walter Besant. James was forty-two in 1884 while Stevenson was eight years younger. He read 'The Art of Fiction' with deep interest and replied to it in an essay called 'A Humble Remonstrance[2], first printed in *Longman's Magazine* (December 1884). Stevenson profoundly disagreed with James as to the nature of the novel and indeed wished to substitute the art of narrative for the art of fiction. Stevenson thought that no art competes with life.

> Man's one method, whether he reasons or creates, is to half-shut his eyes against the dazzle and confusion of reality... Literature, above all, in its most typical mood, the mood of narrative, similarly flees the direct challenge and pursues instead an independent and creative aim.

Differ as they might concerning their concept of fiction, Stevenson and James had much in common, not least that they both possessed the most idealistic motives as to their noble profession as creative artists. Their friendship was the more stimulating that they deeply admired each other's work even as they disagreed about the function of the novel. On his part, Stevenson was immensely flattered that the more experienced James should praise his *Treasure Island* and his admirable style. "It's a luxury, in this immoral age, to encounter someone who *does* write - who is acquainted with that lovely art," James wrote him on December 5th 1884.

Janet Adam Smith has described in her work[3] how James stayed with the Stevensons at Skerryvore from 1885 onwards. When the Stevensons left for America in 1889, the warm friendship endured. Perhaps James with his sensitivity and tact had more understanding of Louis's complex character than most of his friends.

In his relations with Fanny, it was to James's advantage that he had hardly known Louis before his marriage. Fanny always clung to a slight jealousy of his oldest friends, with the exception of Colvin and Baxter. James first came to Bournemouth in late April 1885 to visit his invalid sister Alice to whom he was deeply attached and soon became a frequent visitor to Skerryvore. Louis charmingly commemorates him in a collection of verses[4], *Underwoods*.

> Who comes to-night? We ope the door in vain
> Who comes? My bursting walls, can you contain
> The presences that now together throng
> Your narrow entry, as with flowers and song,
> As with the air of life, the breath of talk
> Lo, how these fair immaculate women walk
> Behind their jocund maker....

Stevenson is referring to James's female characters, mostly more vividly drawn than his own female portraits. One book he disliked intensely was *Portrait of a Lady*, but he praised *Roderick Hudson*.

James usually sat in his own special chair, formerly belonging to Louis's grandfather. Fanny liked him, writing to her mother-in-law that he resembled the Prince of Wales (the future Edward VII) and that she found him "gentle, amiable and soothing". He was finishing *The Bostonians* in Bournemouth. All the same, he called her later "a poor, barbarous and merely instinctive lady".

Louis confided to his new friend that he had occasional tiffs with his wife. He wrote to James from Skerryvore, January 1887:

> My wife is peepy and dowie:** two Scotch expressions
> with which I will leave you to wrestle unaided as a pre-
> paration for my poetical works... It is strange. It is
> strange. We fell out my wife and I the other night; she

** Peepie means fretful or whining. Dowie means mournful, dismal, languid, weak, ailing.

tackled me savagely for being a canary-bird. I replied (bleatingly) protesting that there was no use in turning life into King Lear.

On the whole Adelaide Boodle, a neighbour and friend of Fanny's and Louis's in Bournemouth, gives an intimate and fair account of their lives.[5] She was able to discern the deep sympathy between husband and wife without indulging any illusions. Yet her book has the gushing tone of a woman only too happy to get on friendly terms with such celebrities. Adelaide Boodle greatly admired both Fanny and Louis, describing

> the quiet heroism of Fanny Stevenson's daily and hourly self-restraint. Those erratic moods in which all caution went to the winds must often have tried her nerves almost to breaking-point, but I doubt if she ever allowed him to know what agony she had to live through. She guarded him from every risk, but when she saw that nothing could be gained by remonstrance she quietly said her say and then took refuge in silence.

Louis's temperamental moods made him difficult to live with. Adelaide sensed that he was completely dependent on Fanny and that he submitted most of his writings for her approval. What Miss Boodle and Nellie Sanchez omit to mention is Fanny's hypochondria, possibly increased by the strain of guarding Louis, and causing him anxiety much later in the South Seas.

When Louis learned that Adelaide had literary aspirations, he eventually found time to give her lessons in the art of writing. She truly venerated him. "That frail body of his harboured a soul very like St. Christopher's," she wrote,

> a soul that now and then, at rare intervals, flashed out in a storm of longing to fling his infirmity to the winds and to shoulder the burden of some other weakling whose weariness of body or of mind was but a faint shadow of his own.[6]

112

A man may be highly skilled in the art of writing, but retain a feeble notion of horticulture and fail to distinguish one tree from another. Adelaide Boodle gives a picture of R.L.S. with his long thin hands hacking at the raspberry plants in his garden with a pruning knife and only succeeding in destroying them. No wonder that poor Fanny was so woeful, but she did not blame Louis. "Hush!" she exclaimed. "Louis must never know what he has done. He did it to surprise me, and thinks it has been a splendid day's work." Louis was a poet in his love of trees, but could never tell one wood from another. In his extreme youth Thomas Stevenson had once tried to wean his son from the pursuit of literature by sending him to work under a timber merchant. He was a hopeless pupil.[7]

Fanny became incessantly worried that Louis's health was impaired by the constant visits of his Savile Club friends. Probably the most welcome visitor to Skerryvore was his cousin Bob, and in his society Louis became younger, gayer and more amusing than ever. Occasionally Bob and his family stayed in lodgings in Alum Chine Road. His sister Katharine, unhappily married to a man named de Mattos, came also to Bournemouth. Louis's mother and father now made long visits, increasing the strain for Fanny and Louis, for Thomas Stevenson's health was fast breaking up. Henry James was so upset by the elder Stevensons' insensitive demands on their son and daughter-in-law that he wrote to Colvin, whose mild temper was now exasperated by their conduct. Fanny complained to Colvin in late 1884:

> Louis is ill again, with a dreadful cold ... the very worst one he has ever had with the exception of the one at Nice.... His mother gave it to him in spite of all my entreaties, and went off saying "Now that Louis has entirely recovered his health, we shall expect him to spend his summers with us."

Colvin told Henley (November 30th, 1884), "If ever I am hung it will be for throttling Mrs. T.S. and I shall go smiling and with a good conscience to the gallows."

The Stevensons made interesting friends in Bournemouth. Sir Henry Taylor was now a distinguished old man of eighty-five, descended from a Northumbrian family of scholar-squires, and a retired civil servant in the Colonial Office by profession. He was much older than his southern Irish wife, a woman of remarkable charm and considerable learning and Louis became very fond of her. The Taylors had three sons and two daughters, and Louis mentions one of them, Una, a musician. Although Louis, unlike Bob, had no talent for music, he loved it. He obtained a piano, but merely exasperated his listeners. He wrote to his cousin about his efforts to compose music:

> I had already the key to D Minor. I am sending works daily to Una Taylor. I think it excellent work.... Any time I try to write four parts, madness siezes me. They are so obstinate, so stiff, so mulish, and the world so bubbles over with consecutive fifths.... I lie in bed with a musical slate and labour at four parts till the world goes round me. *O quelle vie, mes amis, O quelle vie!* If you could only hire a piano in bed, but then one would never get up.[8]

There is a picture of Louis in bed with a sheet of music in the South Seas, playing his flageolet. He really needed sympathy for his amateur efforts, but Bob, a skilled musician, poured scorn on them. However, Louis never neglected his work, writing the entire morning.

The Taylors introduced Louis and Fanny to Sir Percy and Lady Shelley. Percy Shelley was son of the poet, and like Stevenson, loved the sea and had a taste for the drama. Jane Shelley even claimed that Louis resembled Percy Shelley so closely he was a reincarnation of the poet. They were both rebels and there was a similarity in the wild restlessness of their characters. Fanny and Louis would sometimes dine with the Shelleys on their estate at Boscombe and attend performances in their private theatre.

Louis dedicated *Underwoods* to his friend Thomas Bodley Scott, his doctor in Bournemouth. He had cause to be grateful to many doctors, including Sir Andrew Clark, "so unwearied in kindness", to Dr. Willey of San Francisco, and to Dr. Karl Ruedi of Davos, "the good genius of the English in his frosty mountains".[9]

Whilst living at Bournemouth, Louis was painted twice by John Singer Sargent, portraits commissioned by Charles Fairchild, an American millionaire.[10] The second portrait painted at Skerry-vore during the summer (1885) is a highly original portrait. In his letter to W.H. Low (October 22, 1885), Stevenson wrote:

> Sargent was down again and painted a portrait of me, walking about in my own dining-room, in my own vel-veteen jacket, and twisting as I go my own moustache; at one corner a glimpse of my wife in an Indian dress, and seated in a chair, that was once my grandfather's.

The picture reveals Louis's restlessness and creative fire. He thought it excellent, but too eccentric to be exhibited.[11]

During their residence in Bournemouth, Louis and Fanny did not often go away, but during the summer of 1885 in their journey to Dartmoor they spent a day or two at Dorchester at the King's Arms Hotel. There they met Thomas Hardy and his wife. Fanny snobbishly wrote of Mrs. Hardy that she was *very* plain, quite underbred and most tedious.[12] "What very strange marriages literary men seem to make," she commented.

At Exeter, Louis was stricken with a violent haemorrhage in his hotel and Fanny had to lift him out of bed many times during the night.

During June 1885 Louis received the very bad news that Professor Fleeming Jenkin, one of his most sage friends, had died on the 12th. He promised Ann Jenkin that he would write an obituary notice for *The Academy*. She must have recalled how impressed she had been at their first meeting in 17 Heriot Row when she called him "a Scots Heine". At Mrs. Jenkin's request he later wrote a *Memoir* of Fleeming Jenkin, a fine biographical work, to be published in 1887.

When in London, Louis would sometimes stay with Sydney Colvin, author of a scholarly book on *John Keats* in the English Men of Letters series. In 1884 Colvin had been appointed to the post of Keeper of the Department of Prints in the British Museum. Memories of those far distant days would besiege Louis in Apemana, in the South Pacific, when homesick for London and for long intimate talks with his friends.

> I heard the pulse of the besieging sea
> Throb far away all night. I heard the wind
> Fly crying and convulse tumultuous palms.
> I rose and strolled. The isle was all bright sand,
> And flailing fans and shadows of the palm.
> To other lands and nights my fancy turned
> To London first and chiefly to your house,
> The many-pillared and the well beloved.

There came to him, "the unsleeping City murmur like a shell, and the muffled tramp of the Museum guard".

Louis would very rarely mention the Bournemouth days later in the South Seas. "Remember the pallid brute that lived in Skerryvore like a weevil in a biscuit," he wrote from Samoa to Henry James. Bournemouth certainly did not restore his health. One fancies that the resort was more congenial to Fanny than to her husband, despite entertaining his inconsiderate friends. It is surprising, therefore, that Louis produced some of his best work there.

Stevenson began writing his famous, topographical novel *Kidnapped* in early 1885, first serialized in *Young Folks* during the summer and later published in book form. Much to the delight of Charles Baxter, Stevenson dedicated it to his old friend. This adventure story is set mostly in the highlands of Scotland in 1751 - a favourite period. The chief character, David Balfour, begins his story, and the simplicity and beauty of language indicative of accomplished art strikes the memory:

> The sun began to shine upon the summit of the hills, as I went down the road, and by the time I had come as far as the manse the blackbirds were whistling in the garden lilacs, and the mist that hung around the valley in the time of the dawn was beginning to arise and die away.

116

There is a memorable picture of Edinburgh when David Balfour on the top of a hill sees "all the country fall away before me down to the sea, and in the midst of this descent, on a long ridge, the city of Edinburgh smoking like a kiln."[13]

There is also evil in this work, in the cruelty and malevolence of David Balfour's Uncle Ebenezer plotting to deprive his nephew of his rightful property. However, Stevenson with his knowledge of human nature realized that no man was altogether evil. Among the seamen of the Brig *Covenant of Dysart*, Balfour found a rough kindness, despite much brutality. Perhaps the characterization of Balfour the Whig and Alan Breck the Jacobite is the finest feature of the book, particularly their adventures as fugitives on the moors and their quarrels. Yet the warm friendship between Balfour and Breck, such contrary characters, is like effulgent sunshine lighting up loch and glen. The narrator tells us:

> He came up to me with open arms, "David," said he, "I love you like a brother." And "O man," he cried in a kind of ecstasy, "am I no a bonny fighter."

When writing his novel, Stevenson made use of his experiences on the island of Mull and the isthmus called the Isle of Erraid, familiar to him when his father wanted him to become a lighthouse engineer.

Another powerful story, *Markheim*, belongs to the Bournemouth period. It clearly reveals the influence of Edgar Allen Poe[14] and Stevenson was familiar with both his stories of terror and his ideas of the *doppelganger* or double.[15] In *Markheim* the main character murders an antique dealer, and the devil makes an appearance as in *Thrawn Janet*, tempting Markheim to further crime, but in the struggle waged by his conscience, he finally resolves to give himself up to the police. *Prince Otto*, a rather artificial story, showing the influence of George Meredith, first appeared in *Longman's Magazine*, April 1885.

Stevenson was always subject to dreams. While asleep "the Brownies" would torment him with all sorts of phantom problems, but according to Fanny, Louis had no difficulty in sleeping at will. One night, however, he experienced a terrible nightmare and his cries of horror caused Fanny to rouse him, much to Louis's anger.

Had he been taking laudanum? "I was dreaming a fine bogey tale," he said reproachfully. Thus was born his famous book *Dr. Jekyll and Mr. Hyde*, one that was to bring him enormous success both in England and America.

Stevenson once wrote to Andrew Lang that he intended to write a story "about a fellow who was two fellows", for he had always held a strong sense of man's double. Perhaps he was familiar with Edgar Allen Poe's stories *William Wilson*, in which he develops the idea of the *doppelganger*, and *Tales of the Grotesque and Arabesque*, both of them written in the 1830s.[16] Another story familiar to Stevenson was Bulwer-Lytton's *A Strange Story*, concerned with doubleness and mesmerism.

The Strange Case of Dr. Jekyll and Mr. Hyde was written in a white heat. For three days Skerryvore was strangely silent as Stevenson worked feverishly on the first draft, containing over 30,000 words. When he read the work to Fanny and Lloyd Osbourne, however, his wife was frankly critical. She considered that he had written a crawler, a tale of sensationalism, when he should have written an allegory. There then ensued a fearful row between husband and wife. Louis returned to his bedroom, to reappear some time later to admit to Fanny that she was right after all. With a dramatic gesture he threw the work into the fire, while they watched shattered as it was consumed by the flames. Here Fanny's critical sense did not fail her, for the manuscript was vastly improved by Louis rewriting it. One can only be amazed by the intense dedication to labour of this ailing man. As Lloyd relates, it was an astounding feat, sixty-four thousand words in six days, more than ten thousand words a day.

Stevenson's strange tale as he conceived it, was based on Gothic Romanticism, and he thought of it as Gothic, but it also reveals his taste for science and the occult. In his early days in Edinburgh, Stevenson had known many scientists, including the father of his friend Sir Walter Simpson, the inventor of chloroform. Many critics have questioned the use of powders by Dr. Jekyll, but Stevenson quaintly explains "that the business of the powders ... is, I am relieved to say, not mine at all but the Brownies," the creatures who spun tales for him as he slept.

Henry Jekyll's full statement of the case explains what he has been doing with the powders and his experimental medicine. It explains the transformation of the benevolent Jekyll into the evil Edward Hyde.

> Even as good shone upon the countenance of the one, evil was written broadly and plainly on the face of the other.... I have observed that when I wore the semblance of Edward Hyde, none would come near to me at first without a visible misgiving of the flesh. This, as I take it, was because all human beings as we meet them, are commingled out of good and evil and Edward Hyde alone in the ranks of mankind was pure evil.[17]

Henry James wrote of his friend's latest book:[18]

> Is *Dr. Jekyll and Mr. Hyde* a work of high philosophic intention, or simply the most ingenious and irresponsible of fictions?... It deals with the relation of the baser parts of man to his nobler - of the capacity for evil that exists in the most generous nature.

Stevenson's real purpose in writing it, was his obsession with duality. The scene of the murder is characteristic of what he described as "fitness in events and places", in virtue of which a given locality becomes associated with an appropriate invented action. The scene is a sordid district of Soho, London on a dark, murky night.

Louis's addiction to opium in early life - he certainly found it beneficial in Mentone when forced to endure pain - was resorted to by many nineteenth century writers. Even Sir Walter Scott, when writing *The Bride of Lammermoor* and suffering intense pain, dictated his manuscript to amanuenses, and was reluctantly obliged to take large doses of laudanum.[19]

Poe's imaginative works, such as the best known *The Fall of the House of Usher*, have several mentions of people addicted to opium. Wilkie Collins, Stevenson's contemporary, writing in the Victorian age has a hero named Franklin Blake in his masterpiece *The Moonstone* (1868) under the influence of opium. Unknown to himself whilst under its influence he takes the moonstone rightly belonging to the daughter of the house. Wilkie Collins, when suffering excruciating pain in his eyes, dictated *The Moonstone* while taking laudanum,[20] but there is no evidence that his creative faculties were impaired.

Stevenson dedicated *Dr. Jekyll and Mr. Hyde* to his cousin Katherine de Mattos, with whom he was on very friendly terms, but their relations were soon to drastically cool. He wrote:

We cannae break the bonds that God decreed to bind,
Still we'll be the children of the heather and the wind,
Far away from home, O, it's still for you and me,
That the broom is blowing bonnie in the North Countrie.

When published in January 1886, the book sold 40,000 copies in the first six months, and the American sales amounted to many thousands more. A preacher in St. Paul's Cathedral used *Dr. Jekyll and Mr. Hyde* as his text. Everywhere the story was discussed.

Lloyd Osbourne now wanted to become a writer. For a while he had studied at Edinburgh University, then stayed with Thomas and Maggie Stevenson at 17 Heriot Row. Lloyd was very shortsighted, needing special spectacles and had continual trouble with his eyes. Though Louis generously encouraged his stepson in his literary aspirations, always ready to give him the wealth of his experience during his apprenticeship, Lloyd really only ever possessed moderate ability. To save his eyes, he learnt to type, but it might well have been better for him to stand on his own feet rather than to bask in the growing literary reputation of his stepfather.

Once while they were living in Bournemouth, Louis and Fanny visited Paris as Will Low's guests. Thomas had generously sent his son a cheque for £100. Both Louis and Fanny enjoyed the two weeks in Paris, but Louis carelessly forgot to cash his father's cheque. When he told Will Low the visit must end, Will naturally puzzled asked "Why?". "Coin" was Louis's laconic reply. Only much later was his mistake discovered.

Towards the end of his sojurn in Bournemouth, Louis became engrossed in the works of Tolstoy, being influenced by his philosophy and self-torturing musings. Tolstoy's tendency, however, to accuse himself for the sins of his youth was far more applicable to Thomas Stevenson than to his son.

Throughout the last few months of his life Thomas Stevenson's health had been worsening, and he finally died at his house in Edinburgh on May 8th 1887. When Louis and Fanny travelled in haste to 17 Heriot Row on May 6th, it was too late.

"Lou arrived this afternoon and his father does not know him," his mother wrote in her diary. His father's death was an overwhelming shock and Louis caught a bad cold with catarrh, so that, owing to his doctor's advice, he was unable to attend the funeral. For three weeks he remained desolate and ill at 17 Heriot Row. Two of his later books are concerned with the difficult relations between fathers and sons, *The Master of Ballantrae* and *Weir of Hermiston*. Although he expected to inherit nothing by his father's will, he was bequeathed £3,000.

Louis now felt that he was no longer under any obligation to remain in Britain. He was attracted to the idea of settling in New Mexico or Colorado and both his doctor in Edinburgh and his doctor in Bournemouth recommended Colorado's mountain air in America as being beneficial for consumptives. One problem was his widowed mother, but Louis and Fanny finally persuaded her to accompany them to America, despite preliminary protests. It was a brave decision on the part of "Maggie" Stevenson to uproot herself from her Edinburgh home and associations and to embark with her son and daughter-in-law on unknown adventures. She was to prove surprisingly adaptable. On Saturday August 20th they finally left Skerryvore to spend two nights at Arnfield's Hotel, near Finsbury Circus, before leaving on *S.S. Ludgate Hill* for New York. Louis siezed the opportunity to see many of his friends, sad encounters many of them, for the last time.

Edmund Gosse relates in *Critical Kitcats*:

> Louis is mourning for his father and he was quite stylishly dressed in a black velvet coat and waistcoat, a black silk neck-tie and dark trousers, so that instead of looking like a Lascar out of employment as he generally does he looked extremely elegant and refined... He prowled about the room in his usual noiseless panther fashion, talking all the time, full of wit and feeling and sweetness, as charming as ever he was, but with a little more sadness and sense of crisis than usual.[21]

It was his last day in Europe.

XII
Saranac and Later

Sidney Colvin came to say farewell to the Stevensons on board the *S.S. Ludgate Hill* before they sailed for America. Little did he know that it was the last time he would ever see Louis. Henry James sent a case of champagne. They were travelling on a tramp steamship, Louis, Fanny, Louis's mother, Lloyd and the French-Swiss maid Valentine Roch, who had been in their service in Bournemouth. Louis wrote later to his cousin Bob from Saranac Lake, New York State:

> I was so happy on board that ship I could not have believed it possible. We had the beastliest weather, and many discomforts, but the mere fact of its being a tramp ship gave us many comforts.... My heart literally sang, I truly care for nothing so much as that.[1]

The boyish adventurer was very prominent in him. At Le Havre a large consignment of horses and monkeys was taken on board, including an ape called Jocko, soon on terms of friendship with Louis.

He went ashore at Le Havre to write a brief note of thanks to Henry James on writing paper headed "Grand Hotel Frascati":

> It is a fine James and a very fine James, and a remarkable fine wine, and as for the boat, it is a damn bad boat, and we are all very rough mariners.

Louis's mother was very game, soon finding her "sea-legs" and a much better sailor than Fanny, who was horribly sick on the *Ludgate Hill*.

Louis was now famous in America, and a stage version of *Dr. Jekyll and Mr. Hyde* was about to attract enormous audiences in New York. He was well known, too, for *Treasure Island* and *Kidnapped*. However, he and his family were taken very much aback by his tumultuous reception on disembarkation, because journalists swarmed about him clamouring for interviews. Will Low was also there at the dock side. What a complete contrast to his dismal experiences in New York eight years ago when his name had been unknown! The editor of *Scribner's* offered Stevenson three thousand five hundred dollars (seven hundred pounds) if he were to write a monthly article for twelve months. Other publishers offered what seemed to him extravagant amounts for various articles. Louis was, by no means, overwhelmed by his success, for he knew how fickle fortune was. He found his reception on the whole embarrassing, and was vastly relieved to take advantage of a cordial invitation from Mr. and Mrs. Fairchild, friends of John Singer Sargent,[2] to stay with them at their summer house at Newport, Rhode Island. There Louis recovered from a bad cold.

The problem for Louis and Fanny was where they were to settle in the immediate future. It was thought that the tiring journey to Colorado would make too great demands on Louis's frail health. Then they heard of a primitive place in the Adirondack mountains in Saranac in Upper New York State where a young New York doctor named Edward Livingstone Trudeau was rapidly acquiring a glowing reputation for treating consumptives. Trudeau had nursed his brother through tuberculosis and had unfortunately himself caught the disease. He established a sanatorium in 1885 and doctors in New York began to send their patients to Saranac. It has not much altered today, but during the fall of 1887 and the long, extremely cold winter when Stevenson lived there, it was a small logging village with its river and lake, now called Lake Placid. It is not far from the Canadian border. Nearby lay Moody Ponds where he loved to skate.

Leaving Louis for the present in Newport, Fanny and Lloyd travelled to Saranac during September, first sailing by steamer up the Hudson for the purpose of finding a suitable house to spend the winter. "Baker's Cottage"*, owned by a typical frontiersman, stood in an elevated situation, above the river, and there could be heard the sound of running water, sure to appeal to Louis.

* It is today a museum, lovingly preserved, containing a large number of Stevenson relics. Its curator is Mike Delehant.

123

It was Baker's job to take parties into the surrounding dense woods for hunting and fishing expeditions. Fanny liked "Baker's Cottage", a white timbered cottage with green shutters and a verandah, and arranged to rent part of it, while Baker and his wife remained in the rear premises. On October 3rd Stevenson, his mother and his family arrived at Saranac when the autumn woods were in their russet glory. Nowhere are they so lovely as during the American fall.

Life was very primitive in "Baker's Cottage". The Stevensons adapted themselves as best they could, aided by their resourceful maid Valentine Roch, a cook, and a boy to chop wood and draw water during the icy winter months. A stove was needed in each bed-chamber and an open fire-place for logs in the main living-room.[3] According to Maggie Stevenson, a very adaptable lady despite her fifty-six years,

> Cold venison was crunching with ice after being an hour in the oven, and I saw a large lump of ice still unmelted in a pot where water was steaming all around it.

Louis wrote to Edmund Gosse on October 8th:

> I am at Saranac Lake in the Adirondacks, I suppose for the winter; ... we have a house in the eye of many winds, with a view of a piece of running water - Highland, all but the dear hue of peat - and of many hills - Highland also, but for the lack of heather. Soon the snow will close on us; ... Sometimes he called it "The Little Switzerland in the Adirondocks".

Saranac reminded both Louis and his mother of the Highlands of Scotland. To William Archer he wrote during October that Fanny was away in Indiana seeing her family;

> my mother, Lloyd and I remain here in the cold, which has been exceeding sharp, and the hill air, which is inimitably fine. We all eat bravely, and sleep well, and make great fires and get along like one o'clock.[4]

As was his habit, he smoked like a chimney, rolling his own cigarettes. In the mantelpiece over the fireplace are cigarette burns made by Stevenson.

We can imagine the dauntless Louis, now aged almost thirty-seven, dressed in a buffalo coat, astrakan cap and Indian boots, sallying forth for his daily walk. It is evident that he found the clear, sparkling air beneficial for some of his finest creative writing. On the whole he stood the cold better than other members of his family. To Henry James he wrote during October of the joy of running water:

> I like water ... either running swiftly among stones, or else largely qualified with whisky. As I write, the sun (which has been long a stranger) shines in at my shoulder; from the next room, the bell of Lloyd's typewriter makes an agreeable music as it patters off (at a rate which astonishes this experienced novelist) the early chapters of a humorous romance (Lloyd was writing the first draft of *The Wrong Box* or as it was originally called, *The Finsbury Tontine*); from still further off ... rumours of Valentine about the kitchen stove come to my ears.[5]

Fanny and Louis had let Skerryvore when they went to America, and had left Adelaide Boodle, "their gamekeeper" as he nicknamed her, to keep an eye on their interests. Louis wrote to her from Saranac Lake in December, telling her that the place did not suit his wife's health:

> It is my private opinion that no place does. She has gone to New York for a change, leaving my mother and me and Valentine alone in our wind-beleaguered hilltop hat-box of a house. You should hear the cows butt against the walls in the early morning while they feed.

Fanny was ill again in "Baker's Cottage" in March 1888.

At Saranac Louis was planning one of the most important of his books, *The Master of Ballantrae*, and indeed began part of it there. He mentions it in a letter dated December 24th, 1887, to Sidney Colvin, including the dramatis personae:

> My old Lord Durrisdeer, the Master of Ballantrae and Henry Durie, his sons, Clementina (her name was changed to Alison), Ephraim MacKellar, land steward at Durrisdeer and narrator of most of the book, and Francis Burke, Chevalier de St. Louis, one of Prince Charles Edward's Irishmen.[6]

Where did Stevenson find the surname for his chief narrator MacKellar? He liked to visit churchyards, and in the sweet little village of Kirkmichael in Perthshire where he once stopped at the inn for lunch, there is a tombstone which reads:

IN MEMORY OF
THE LATE
ALEXANDER MACKELLAR
FOR 17 YEARS
MINISTER IN THIS PARISH
DIED 1866

Who can say? A Stevenson devotee, David Angus, suggested this.

The idea for the book came to Louis much earlier in his life when he was twenty-five. On a walking tour through Carrick and Galloway he passed through Ballantrae, a place he stowed away in his capacious memory for future use.[7] Now twelve years later at the age of thirty-seven, Stevenson in his primitive dwelling outside the hamlet of Saranac found the conditions most congenial for embarking on the novel taking him to Scotland, parts of India (a country he never visited) and America. "I was walking one night on the verandah," relates Louis.

> It was winter, the night was very dark, the air extraordinary clear and cold, and sweet with the purity of forests. From a good way below, the river was to be heard contending with ice and boulders ...

The sense of isolation struck him as ideal for the making of a story.[8]

Stevenson's characters, the Master of Ballantrae (James), a very devil, and his younger brother Henry Durie are brilliantly drawn, and their mutual hatred is portrayed in a masterly fashion. The relations of the old Lord with his favourite sons James and Henry are skillfully depicted, based on Stevenson's own complicated relations with his father. What was far more difficult for Stevenson was to provide a convincing portrait of MacKellar, the land steward at Durrisdeer, for to make a narrator really alive is fraught with difficulty, but Stevenson succeeds with MacKellar, whose ultimate loyalty is to the House of Durrisdeer rather than to 'Mr. Henry'. In *The Master of Ballantrae*, Stevenson is again obsessed with evil, but the character of the older brother, who serves with Prince Charles Edward in the '45 is not wholly bad, for he had courage and was cultured. However, the female sex are often attracted to complete scoundrels!

The best parts of the book are the beginning and the celebrated duel fought at night by the light of candles between the Master and Mr. Henry. When Henry strikes James in the mouth,

> the Master sprang to his feet like one transfigured; I had never seen the man so beautiful. "A blow," he cried. "I would not take a blow from God Almighty!"

There is nobility in the book, even greatness in parts, but the ending is feeble and Stevenson admitted much later in the Pacific that "This cursed end of *The Master* hangs over me like the gallows." While Henley thought the book grimy, Louis thought it grim and tragic.

Stevenson's strength as a writer did not extend to his portrayal of female characters, with the exception of the two Kirsties in *Weir of Hermiston* - his last unfinished work. These are magnificent creations. Another female character portrayed with simplicity and sympathy is Uma, the native girl in *The Beach of Falesá*, his finest story of the South Seas, but it was a later work. Perhaps his love of Polynesia made it easier for him to describe a typical native woman.

On the other hand Alison Durie in *The Master of Ballantrae* is an insipid character who never really comes alive. It would seem that Stevenson, so unlike the Victorians in his abhorrence of respectability and humbug, was curiously restricted in his literary work by what has been described as the prurient prudery of popular taste. Was it the influence of his dead Victorian father? or possibly Fanny? Stevenson could rarely write about sex in a natural way. The female characters in Wilkie Collins' *The Moonstone*, such as Rachel Verinder with her self-willed nature and secret passions, and Rosanna the wretched servant girl, are much more convincingly portrayed. Isabel Archer in Henry James's *Portrait of a Lady* is also a very clever creation.

E.L. Burlingame, the editor of Scribner's, made an offer for the serialisation of *The Master of Ballantrae* and Stevenson promised to send him the opening chapters. In the course of the winter, however, he was writing to him, *"The Master of Ballantrae* I have had to leave aside, as I was quite worked out." It was eventually completed in Honolulu in 1888-89. Burlingame became a fairly constant correspondent.

Louis wrote to his cousin Bob from Saranac: "Wealth is only useful for two things. A yacht and a string quartette. For these I would sell my soul." He was never happy for long, away from the sea. During the long winter months at Baker's Cottage, the Stevenson family, shivering with cold, talked longingly about a voyage in the Pacific. A new literary acquaintance of Louis's, an editor in New York named Sam McClure, was keen on the idea of Louis chartering a yacht to be paid for by the author writing monthly letters. For the purpose of making inquiries about a suitable yacht, Fanny left Saranac, during March 1888, for San Francisco to see her daughter Belle Strong and her sister Nellie Sanchez.

Shortly after Fanny's departure, Louis received a letter from Henley, which came as a thunderbolt to him, a dreadful shock. Written from Chiswick on March 9th 1888, it mostly consisted of a loud lament about Louis's absence in America. "Why the devil do you go and bury yourself in that bloody country of dollars and spew?" he tactlessly asked. The letter was marked "Private and Confidential". One passage accused Fanny of plagiarism and Louis, completely loyal to his wife, could not stomach such an insult.

"I read *The Nixie* with considerable amazement," he wrote:

> It's Katharine, surely, it's Katharine's? The situation, the environment, the principal figure - *voyons!* There are even reminiscences of phrases and imaginary, parallel incidents - *que sais-je?* It is all better focussed, no doubt, but I think it has lost as much at least as it has gained, and why there wasn't a double signature is what I've not been able to understand.

Henley ended his letter, "Forgive this babble, and take care of yourself, and *burn this letter*."[9] Louis, however, kept the letter.

The Nixie was a short story by Fanny, published by Scribner during March, about a young man's encounter with a nixie (or fairy) in his compartment on a train. The Katharine referred to in Henley's letter was Bob's sister Katharine de Mattos, Louis's first cousin. Katharine had originally written a short story, but it differed from Fanny's in that there was no nixie, merely a girl recently escaped from a lunatic asylum.[10] Both Katharine and Fanny had certainly discussed Katharine's story when she was staying at Skerryvore, but she had been unsuccessful in getting a publisher for it and had suggested that Fanny should write her version of the story.

Louis's letters to Henley on the subject are in the National Library of Scotland, pretty well known. It was surely a mistake for Louis to tell Fanny about Henley's letter knowing her likely reaction. It was not the first time he had quarrelled with this friend, whom he had known for thirteen years, for both men had faults, Louis's irascible temper and Henley's lack of consideration. Henley had several motives for writing his letter, his dislike of Fanny, who had objected once again to his over-exuberance and boisterousness in tiring her beloved and ailing husband at Skerryvore when they were collaborating together in writing plays. There was also an element of jealousy in Henley's relationship with Louis, for the latter was now far more successful than his friend, occasionally lent him money, and Henley always suspected, with some justification, that Louis had never wholeheartedly collaborated with him when writing *Deacon Brodie* and his other plays. *Deacon Brodie* had only enjoyed minor success in America, indeed, when on tour might even be considered a failure. Henley's younger brother Teddy, an actor by profession, had the leading part in the play, but had exasperated Stevenson by his drunken habits and his inclination to indulge in tavern brawls.

To a man of Louis's hypersensitive temperament, Henley's disloyalty could hardly be forgiven. He wrote:

> My dear Henley (no longer Dear Lad, his usual form)
> I write with indescribable difficulty, and if not with perfect temper, you are to remember how very rarely a husband is expected to receive such accusations against his wife. I can only direct you to apply to Katharine and ask her to remind you of that part of the business which took place in your presence and which you seem to have forgotten. ...
>
> From the bottom of my soul I believe what you wrote to have been merely reckless words written in forgetfulness with no clear appreciation of their meaning, but it is hard to think that anyone - and least of all my friend - should have been so careless of dealing agony....
>
> You will pardon me if I can find no form of signature, I pray God such a blank will not be of long endurance.[11]

Although there was a temporary reconciliation, the friendship was never the same again.

Henley wrote to Louis:

> Your letter is heart-breaking. You may blame me in the bitterest terms for the cruel blunder I made in opening my mind to you, and I shall not complain for I deserve them all. I should, I know now, have said nothing and I shall never cease from regretting that I gave you this useless, this unnecessary pain. You must believe though that I did not strike to hurt ...

Deeply troubled, Louis confided in his old friend Charles Baxter, who was also a friend of Henley's. During March, Louis wrote: "I fear I have come to an end with Henley." He had helped him with money, with service,

... and yet the years come, and every year there is a fresh
outburst against me.... I can't say it is anger that I feel,
but it is despair. My last reconciliation with Henley is
not yet a year old, and here is the devil again. I am weary
of it all - weary, weary, weary. And this letter was (so
the writer said) intended to cheer me on a sick-bed! My
God deliver me from such consolations, I slept but once
last night and then woke in an agony, dreaming I was
quarrelling with you. The miserable cold day was creep-
ing in, and I remembered you were the last of my old
friends with whom I could still say I was still on the old
terms. I have not changed my thoughts of him, not even,
I believe my heart.... The old intimacy is impossible on
the old terms.[12]

Baxter replied in an extremely tactful letter, saying that he refused
to believe that Henley had wilfully intended to hurt Louis or Fanny.
He thought Henley was irritated over the lack of success of the
plays, and that Louis's gifts of money to Henley's family had made
too bitter a contrast between success and failure.

A man of a less passionate nature would not have been so
powerfully affected by Henley's extreme tactlessness, but Stevenson could not condone what seemed to him a conspiracy against
him by Henley and his circle of women friends. When Louis wrote
to his cousin Katharine taxing her with a dreadful, preconceived
plot, Katharine de Mattos (her marriage had been a failure) replied:

I know this can *never* get better, but perhaps nothing
can get worse. I don't think I exaggerate when I say I
was saddened with despair when I read your letter....
I can only myself know how impossible it would have
been to me to do such a thing.

Fanny's reaction in San Francisco was entirely predictable. She
raved against Louis's English friends, particularly Henley, saying
that she never wished to see England again. With the exception of
Sidney Colvin and Charles Baxter, she had never loved Louis's English friends. As for Henley, henceforward he harboured resentment
against Louis.

131

Colvin, who was in possession of the true facts, sided with Fanny. He later wrote:[13]

> With reference to the cause of estrangement and in the end actual quarrel between Stevenson's widow and his sometime close friend William Ernest Henley, it ought to be publicly known that the wife had ample and just cause for regarding the friendship as one that entailed risks to Louis's health and should be discouraged accordingly. For all his crippled bodily condition, Henley was in talk the most boisterously untiring, the lustiest and most stimulating of companions and could never bring himself to observe the consideration due to Louis's frail health and impaired lungs. Anxiety on this account was the main cause of the wife's disliking his society for her husband.

He knew from his own experience that Fanny did not hold the kind of jealousy which a wife commonly feels towards the friends of her husband's bachelor days. She was, however, capable of injured feelings where her husband's friends were concerned.

Louis was very glad to leave Saranac and to go to New York, where he spent a fortnight in the latter part of April. He was with his mother, Lloyd and Valentine, for Fanny was still searching for a suitable yacht in San Francisco. Will Low, his artist friend, now suggested that Louis should go to Manasquan, New Jersey, and there he went with his stepson Lloyd. He spent a happy, leisurely month in Union House, a delightful country inn reminding him of the villages around Fontainebleau. He wrote to Colvin during May:

> We are here, a cat-boat at our disposal, the sea always audible on the outer beach, the lagoon as smooth as glass, all the little queer, many coloured villas standing shuttered and empty....

Will Low came on a visit, together with a celebrated French sculptor, Augustus St. Guadens, an admirer of Stevenson's writings, who had worked on a medallion before he had gone to Saranac.

Louis immediately made friends with young Homer St. Gaudens, who accompanied his father.

While Louis remained at Manasquan, yearning for a sea voyage, a telegram suddenly arrived from Fanny announcing that she had found a yacht, the *Casco*, suitable for a cruise in the South Pacific. Louis immediately sent a return telegram, giving his approval to the project of chartering her. "Blessed girl, take the yacht and expect us in ten days - Lou."[14]

XIII

Travels in the South Pacific

In vain Louis had sought for many years a climate to suit his health where his life might be prolonged. The owner of the yacht *Casco* was Dr. Merritt, an eccentric and very rich man. It was by no means easy to persuade him to agree to hiring out the yacht, for he had a slight prejudice against literary men in general and publicity regarding Louis in the local San Francisco papers had not all been favourable. The captain of the vessel was named Otis. The *Casco* was a beautiful little vessel, ninety-five feet in length and with a seventy-ton burthen. She had white sails and white decks, and her cabin fittings were of silk and velvet. She was kept so spotlessly clean by her crew that she was later known as "the silver ship" by the people of the 'cotal' atoll of Fakarava.

Louis might write to the faithful Baxter that he went on his journey with a bitter heart, haunted by Henley's letter, but he intended all the same to have a good time on the *Casco*. While Louis rested in the Occidental Hotel, Fanny and her mother-in-law bought provisions for a long voyage. Fanny's health was causing Louis anxiety, for she had to endure an operation for the removal of a growth in her throat.

When Captain Otis met Louis at the house of Dr. Merritt, in Oakland, he was not particularly impressed. "Imagine," he wrote,

> a man of medium height, so painfully thin that his clothes seemed a burden to him, his brown hair falling to his shoulders around a face of death like whiteness, but alight with the most fascinating brown eyes I had ever seen.[1]

Louis, not yet aged thirty-eight. Captain Otis had only read one of Stevenson's works, *Treasure Island*.

The family eagerly anticipated the sea journey to the South Seas, even Maggie in her white widow's cap and black and white lawn dress was excited. For Louis the woof of his life was filled with a strange magic, and enchantment, gazing up at skies at night aglow with stars, larger and brighter than anywhere else. That was his vision of the South Seas, and his experiences would colour and influence his writings on the Pacific, such as *The Ebb-Tide, The Beach of Falesá, The South Seas* and *The Wrecker*. Louis was to pass the last six years of his life in the Pacific, never to return to Europe.

On June 26th 1888, Louis, Fanny, Maggie Stevenson, Lloyd Osbourne and Valentine, their faithful French-Swiss servant, embarked on the *Casco*, while Fanny's daughter Belle, Mrs. Virgil Williams and other friends gave them a tremendous send-off from the wharf. It was curious that the *Casco* was at first undermanned, having a crew of only four men, which would have meant the Captain being the only real navigator aboard, definitely a potential hazard if the yacht was to encounter Pacific squalls.

Louis, always studied voraciously the histories of the countries he was about to visit. Having made the acquaintance of Charles Warren Stoddart, through an introduction provided by Dora Williams when he was living in Bush Street, San Francisco, he learnt much, for Stoddart was an experienced writer and traveller in the South Seas. He had interested Louis in the works of Herman Melville, and in his own book *South Sea Idyll*.

The *Casco* first made for the Marquesan Islands, which lay eight degrees south of the Equator, then under the domination of the French. However, before these islands had been sighted, a sudden "freak spell', described by Captain Otis as "black as a black cat", descended on the *Casco*, and for a time Louis and his family were in considerable danger, exhilarating perhaps for him, but terrifying for Fanny and the others.

Even a hardened traveller such as Stevenson was enraptured as the faint outline of an island came into view. Nuka-hiva lay ahead and the *Casco* anchored in Anaho Bay. It was July 21st and for Louis it was fascinating to watch as a tattooed native chief and a swarm of scantily dressed Polynesians clambered about the vessel. From the first, Louis was favourably impressed by the

Polynesians, and learnt to love them, hardly able to distinguish their faults. He wrote to Colvin:

> I chose these isles as having the most beastly population, and they are far better and far more civilized than me. I know one old chief Ko-o-amua, a great cannibal in his day, who ate his enemies, even as he walked home from killing 'em, and he is a perfect gentleman, and exceedingly amiable and simple-minded: no fool, though.

Louis was always their champion, but may have been blinded by prejudice.

In the lush, mountainous Marquesan islands Louis's health made a remarkable recovery. He described the effect of this first island landfall on his mind in his book *In the South Seas*. He was also keeping a diary, to form the basis of travel-letters he intended to send Sam McClure in New York. For physical exercise, he would ride a horse for long hours. Both Louis and Fanny noticed how happy the Marquesans were, and even "Aunt Maggie" began to wonder whether European missionary activities in Polynesia really benefitted the natives.

After six weeks on the Marquesas, the Stevensons sailed south-eastwards on the *Casco* making for Tahiti, intending to disembark at Fakarava on the way. Whilst at sea, Louis was lying awake on September 16th courting sleep in the open air cockpit, when he experienced a strange vision of Drummond Street in Edinburgh. He wrote Charles Baxter:

> There was nothing visible but the Southern stars, and the steersman there out by the binnacle lamp; we were looking forward to a most deplorable landfall on the morrow, praying God we should fetch a tuft of palms, which are to indicate the Dangerous Archipelago; the night was as warm as milk.[2]

Louis remembered the days of long ago when he picked about Rutherfords, so familiar to students, and feared that he would make a mere shipwreck of his life. What an extraordinary transformation there had been! In the warm Pacific night, Edinburgh with its biting east wind pervaded his mind. He wrote his "dear Charles" that he was avid to write a fine book of travels and tell more of the South Seas. Little was known, "except Herman Melville, perhaps, who is a howling cheese" (a favourite phrase). Melville indeed provides a marvellous, if sometimes fictional, account of the life and savage customs of the Marquesans in 1842, in his popular work *Typee*[3], but his imaginative gifts made him prone to romanticize. Perhaps Stevenson was attracted by Melville to the evil and fear lurking beneath the innocent and idyllic native life. Both writers possessed the Calvinistic sense of Innate Depravity and Original Sin.

To Colvin he wrote on September 21st, signing his name "The Old Man Virulent", alluding to his fits of uncontrollable temper he was subject to in youth. He asks him to give his kind love to Henley, to Henry James and to any other friends. Much as he loved the sea, Louis had no illusions about it. A month later he was writing to Colvin saying that the voyage had given him more strength than he thought possible.

> And yet the sea is a terrible place, stupefying to the mind, and poisonous to the temper, the sea, the motion, the lack of space, the cruel publicity, the villainous tinned foods, the sailors, the captain, the passengers.[4]

Indeed the voyage to Fakarava where the Stevenson family arrived on September 4th, was not only difficult, but dangerous. There they were enchanted by the tropical nights and the moon shining on the mysterious palm trees. They would listen spell-bound to the stories of the half-Tahitian, half-French, Monsieur Donat Rimareau, as he related the islands' legends, and various psychic stories. In his turn, Louis would narrate Scottish legends and store in his memory the legends of Fakarava, to be used in his short story *The Isle of Voices*.[5] Fanny recalled the wonderful moonlight and the cocoa palms much later in her life.

For most people, Tahiti represents their impression of an idyllic place, but Louis when he arrived at Papeete, its principal town, had a very severe cold. There, Louis and his family found a little wooden house surrounded by mangoes. He did not care for Papeete. The French Captain Louis de Bougainville had landed in 1768 shortly after Captain James Cook and had been enchanted by the sensual, laughing brown-skinned girls, who had clambered naked over the side of his ship to the delight of his crew. Gauguin[6] also arrived in Tahiti in 1890 soon after Stevenson, a surly, rude artist to be the model for Somerset Maugham's Charles Strickland in *The Moon and Sixpence*, for he had spent several weeks there in February 1917.

Stevenson saw enough of Papeete, the French colonial capital, to sense the decadence of its floating, white population, demoralized and aimless. He was ill with incipient haemorrhage, and in his novel *The Ebb-Tide* he introduces his three corrupt male characters, the drunken sea-Captain Davis, Herrick, a failure and the vicious, vulgar Huish, on the beach at Papeete. *The Ebb-Tide* was begun in collaboration with Lloyd Osbourne, but Louis continued it, on his own, later in Samoa. In Chapter IX, Stevenson describes an island dinner, remarkable for its variety: "Turtle-soup and steak, fish, fowls, a sucking pig, a coconut salad, and sprouting coconut roasted for dessert".

Louis and his family decided to move on in the *Casco* to Taravo in the south of Tahiti, and from thence, in a wagon owned by a Chinese, to the village of Tautira, and he fell in love with it. He was not sorry when Captain Otis discovered that the mainmast of the vessel had dry rot, for it entailed a longer stay at Tautira. To Baxter, he wrote on November 10th: "Tautira is first chop" and enclosed some well known verses, included in *Songs of Travel*. Here is the first verse:

> Home no more home to me,
>> Whither must I wander?
> Hunger my driver, I go where I must.
> Cold blows the winter wind over hill and heather;
> Thick drives the rain, and my roof is in the dust.
> Loved of wise men was the shade of my roof-tree,
> The true word of welcome was spoken in the door -
> Dear days of old, with the faces in the firelight,
> Kind folks of old, you come again no more.

Louis was very ill with congestion of the lungs in Tautira, but in this idyllic place slowly recovered his health, so that his mother wrote to her sister that she had not seen him look so well since 1879. According to Fanny, "Aunt Maggie" often went barefoot "and never, I believe, wears stockings".

Fanny happily wrote a long letter to Colvin on December 4th saying that a beautiful brown Princess - it was Princess Moe, ex-Queen of Raiatea[7], had befriended them. She had insisted that the whole party should come and stay as her guests in the house of her relation, the sub-chief Ori a Ori. Fanny thought that Ori looked very like a Roman Emperor in Bronze. In some respects he reminded her of a Colonel of the Guards. When Princess Moe gave a lavish feast her guests wore wreaths of golden yellow leaves as was the custom. According to Fanny, Princess Moe saved Louis's life, feeding him on fresh mullet cooked in coconut milk, lime juice and red pepper. Fanny told Colvin that Louis was working hard on his new story *The Master of Ballantrae*, and had almost finished it. He was also engrossed in writing two of his long narrative poems, *The Ballad of Rahero*, based on a legend of the Tivas, the people of Tautira, and *The Feast of Famine*, a story about the Marquesas. These ballads are exciting stories in which Stevenson excelled, but Colvin did not approve of them and he seldom appreciated Stevenson's best work done in the South Seas. Louis called Tautira "the garden of the world".

Fanny describes a typical, native lunch of raw fish with sauce made of coconut milk mixed with sea water and lime juice, roasted Taro poipoi and bananas with coconut cream.

At last the mainmast of the *Casco* was repaired, and the travellers were ready to sail from Tahiti to Honolulu on Christmas Day, 1888. Everybody wept, sad at departure from Tautira, and the tall, handsome Ori was in tears. Louis thought him "one of the finest creatures extant". So Louis, Fanny, Aunt Maggie, Lloyd and Valentine embarked on their vessel, unaware of the further dangers about to assail them.

Safely arrived in Honolulu, Louis wrote his cousin Bob during February 1889 of the hazards that had confronted them. The voyage lasted a month.

We had been nearly twelve hours beating off the lee shore of Eimeo (or Moorea, next island to Tahiti) in half a gale of wind with a violent head sea.... We ran out of food, and were quite given up for lost in Honolulu.

His stepdaughter Belle, then living there with her husband Joe Strong, was waiting to greet her mother and Louis, but people tactfully refrained from mentioning the *Casco*. "One stirring day," Louis told Bob,

> was that in which we sighted Hawaii.... The swell, the heaviest I have ever been out in - I tried in vain to estimate the height, *at least* fifteen feet, came tearing after us about a point and a half off the wind. We had the best hand - old Louis - at the wheel, and really he did nobly, and had noble luck, for it never caught us once.

Captain Otis records, ten years later, that Stevenson never turned a hair. He told the captain that it was a new experience and a desirable one. With sparkling eyes, he promised to find a place for it in his writings, and he used the experience in *The Wrecker*.

Belle, Joe and their son Austin, aged eight, eagerly welcomed Fanny and Louis to Honolulu harbour in late January 1889. The Strongs now arranged that Stevenson should be presented to the native King David Kalakaua of Hawaii, a man of considerable intelligence, but autocratic and debauched.

Louis indeed arrived in Hawaii at a critical stage in her history when the USA were planning annexation of Hawaii as an independent kingdom. Undoubtedly Kalakaua foresaw the consequences of American policy, and as a traditionalist did his utmost to preserve Hawaii's ancient customs, organizing a secret society, the *Hale Nuau*[8] for Hawaiians pledged to do so. In the early 1880s Kalakaua's ambition had been to gather all the cognate races on the Pacific into a mighty Polynesian Confederacy over which he would rule. Louis listened to his opinions and was somewhat influenced, though he had been warned about the King's ambivalent character.

He was extremely convivial, thinking nothing of drinking five or six bottles of champagne (Louis's wine store in the *Casco*) before dinner and he was especially partial to brandy. Whatever his serious faults, Stevenson found Kalakaua amiable enough, but he confided to Baxter in a letter written on March 8th: "Kalakaua is a terrible companion; a bottle of fizz is like a glass of sherry to him; he thinks nothing of five or six in an afternoon as a whet for dinner." He confided in Baxter that he was toiling like a galley slave, rewriting *The Wrong Box*, a book in which Lloyd had collaborated, and completing *The Master of Ballantrae*, later at Waikiki. Still uncertain of his future plans, Louis was playing with the idea of settling in Madeira, but it came to nothing.

There were two parties in Hawaii, the King's party, a doubtful majority of natives after 1887, a minority of whites and a reform party consisting partly of natives and a majority of the whites. Very bitter sentiments existed between the two groups. By 1889 Kalakaua had been compelled to grant a new constitution in which various abuses and scandals had to be remedied, but the monarchy was to survive for only four more years. Kalakaua was very keen to get the support of Stevenson, an influential writer and foreigner, at this period of stress as he was already known as an ardent lover of Polynesians.

Louis and Fanny rented a small house on Waikiki Beach, three miles from Honolulu, with a garden of oleanders, and with a hut in which he worked. For recreation he swam off the magnificent Waikiki Beach, and sometimes played his flageolet in bed. There at Waikiki, King Kalakaua and other friends would visit him and discuss Samoan politics, for in 1889 the Americans, the British and the Germans were interested in Samoa as a strategic base. Stevenson had been interested in the islands, off Samoa, since June 1875, when a New Zealander had first talked about them at 17 Heriot Row.

Louis soon formed a quixotic desire to defend the Polynesians of Samoa from the aggression of foreigners. It was in February that he wrote a strongly critical letter to *The Times*, in London, about the present extraordinary state of affairs on that island. He did not know then that he would spend the last four years of his life in Samoa.

There were lighter moments. It was whilst staying in Hawaii Louis fell in love with a beautiful Princess Kaiulani, aged thirteen, niece of King Kalakaua. She was daughter of Archibald Cleghorn, a Scots neighbour of Louis's living near Waikiki, and Princess Miriam Likelike, the King's sister, now dead. There still stands the imposing banyan tree where Louis often came to greet the little dark Princess and to tell her stories. Her father lived at Ainahau near Louis's home. One can only hope that her fear of her forthcoming journey to Britain to be educated there might have been lessened by Stevenson's attentions. He mentions her in a letter to Will Low on May 20th (1890):[9]

If you want to cease to be a republican, see my little Kaiulani as she goes through - but she is gone already. You will die a red: I wear the colours of that little royal maiden.

On her departure he wrote some charming verses to her:

> Forth from her land to mine she goes,
> The island maid, the island rose,
> Light of heart and bright of face
> The daughter of a double race.
> Her islands here in Southern sun,
> Shall mourn their Kaiulani gone,
> And I, in her dear banyan shade
> Look vainly for my little maid.
> But our Scots Islands far away
> Shall glitter with unwonted day,
> And cast for once their tempests by
> To smile in Kaiulani's eye.

Written in April to Kaiulani, in the April of her age, and at Waikiki, within easy walk of Kaiulani's banyan.

There is a picture of her in the Silverado Museum in St. Helena, California. Kai'ulani had a very sad life. After her aunt Lili'uokalani succeeded King Kalakaua as Queen, she was soon deposed by an American coup d'etat. In 1898, America annexed Hawaii, despite the protests of the young Princess Kai'ulani. She died at twenty-six, mourned by Hawaians.

In 1889 there were changes in the Stevenson household. Louis's mother Maggie went home to Scotland as she wanted to see her ailing sister, intending to rejoin Louis later in Samoa. Valentine Roch was eventually given notice by Fanny. The reason for this drastic decision was owing to Valentine's affair with a sailor on the *Casco*, natural enough for such an attractive girl, who had given the Stevensons six years loyal service. Valentine returned to California, to be married. Fanny, however, got on especially well with their excellent Chinese cook Ah Fu, who was devoted to her, giving her loyal service on the *Casco* and at Waikiki. Fanny wrote of him that he had as strong a sense of romance as Louis himself.

142

XIV

The Road to Valhalla

Fanny was always convinced that she knew best the kind of book Louis should write, and in her role as helpful critic, she had often given him invaluable advice, but by 1889 during their travels in the South Pacific she did not realize how fully her husband had matured as a writer. His aims were bigger, more ambitious; he did not want to establish his reputation as a mere story teller, great though he was, rather to write an objective account emphasizing the unique character of the South Sea islands, providing significant portraits of the personalities he encountered. He thought of himself more as a historian, and his approach to the book he had in mind was objective and even factual, rather than subjective. The trouble was most of his readers expected him to continue to write a travel book in the same vein as his third book, *Travels with a Donkey*, written with a graceful and delicate charm, revealing much of his egocentric self, or his early book *An Inland Voyage*. He was older now, more mature, less dependent on Fanny, because of his vastly improved health, though deeply attached and grateful to her. She was right, however, in thinking it would not be a commercial success.

His book *In the South Seas*, written mostly in 1890, was only published two years after Louis's death, but it was criticized for its dullness. Even Colvin, who knew nothing about the South Seas, considered it dull, but to an unprejudiced reader today, it is a fully mature, wise book full of sentiment, observation and understanding, containing portraits of native kings such as Tembinoka[1] of the Gilbert Islands and rich in characterization. It may lack the charm of his earlier travel books, but it is more profound. If Stevenson lacks sufficient intellectual power to make it a real success, he makes a gallant and sincere effort to achieve it. His series of South Seas letters, syndicated and commissioned by McClure for the New York *Sun*, were not much appreciated, and after thirty-four of those letters had been published the paper wanted to terminate the contract.

Fanny appealed to Colvin in a letter written from Honolulu (May 21st, 1889):

> Louis has the most enchanting material ... and I am afraid he is going to spoil it all. He has taken into his Scotch Stevenson head that a stern duty lies before him, and that his book must be a sort of scientific and historical impersonal thing.... Think of a small treatise on the Polynesian races being offered to people who are dying to hear about Ori a Ori, the making of brothers with cannibals, the strange stories they told and the extraordinary adventures that befell us.... What a thing it is to have "a man of genius" to deal with. It is like managing an overbred horse.

Louis had yet to achieve the summit of his imaginative genius, but was Fanny in her roles of managing wife and literary critic and her requests to Colvin to throw the weight of his influence on the scales with her, really acting in his best interests? Louis's own intuition and bizarre wanderings would tell him the road to follow. Fanny told Colvin that Louis was now a new man, never a sign of haemorrhage. This very day he had gone to visit Molokai, the leper island in Hawaii.

It was an extremely brave action on Stevenson's part, revealing his character in its most favourable light, a dangerous challenge. He described the experience in a letter to his wife, and to James Payn, his old friend, Editor of the *Cornhill Magazine*. He wrote: "No stranger time have I ever had, nor any so moving."[2] Hypersensitive Louis was horrified by the sufferings of the lepers he encountered, but there was a moral loveliness. When he saw these dread creatures smile and look happy, all horror was gone from him. He was swept by beautiful emotions. He described the leper promontory at Kalawao in his letter to Fanny:

> Lowland, quite bare and bleak and harsh, a little town of wooden houses, two churches, a landing-stair, all unsightly, sour, northerly, lying athwart the sunrise, with the great wall of the pali cutting the world out on the south.[3]

144

He was deeply impressed by the self-sacrifice of the nuns, who devoted their lives to the patients. He told Fanny:

> Every hand was offered: I have gloves, but I had made up my mind on the boat's voyage *not* to give my hand, that seemed less offensive than the gloves.

Louis generously gave the inmates a new croquet set and offered to teach them. They found it incredible that the author did not shrink from them and shun them as was the custom among white men, according to Sister Leopoldina, one of the nuns.[4] Louis later enclosed a poem to the Matron of the Bishop House, Kalapa:

> To see the infinite pity of this place,
> The mangled limb, the devastated face,
> The innocent sufferer smiling at the rod,
> A fool was tempted to deny his God.
> He sees, and shrinks. But if he look again,
> Lo, beauty springing from the breast of pain!
> He marks the Sisters on the painful shores,
> And even a fool is silent and adores.

"The poetry is in the pity" as Wilfred Owen, the great Welsh poet, once wrote.

Whilst in Kalawao, Louis heard much about Father Damien, the devoted Belgian priest who had recently died of leprosy. The more Stevenson learnt of Damien's defects of character, the more highly he regarded him. He wrote to Colvin during June from Honolulu: Damien

> was dirty, bigoted, untruthful, unwise, tricky, but superb with generosity, residual candour and fundamental good humour.... A man, with all the grime and paltriness of mankind, but a saint and hero all the more for that.[5]

Many months later when Louis was in Sydney, Australia, he was furious when he read in a church journal a denunciation of Damien by the Rev. Dr. Hyde of Honolulu. It aroused all his chivalry, hatred of hypocrisy and lack of Christian charity. Memories of his Calvinistic beliefs fused with memories of his early struggles to understand Christian ethics. All the same it was rash of Louis to send his counterblast and strong defence of Damien, published in the *Australian Sun*, using such libellous expressions that he fully expected the writer of the letter, Dr. Hyde, a Presbyterian minister, to sue him for libel. Fortunately he refrained from doing so.

Stevenson tells us in his book *The South Seas* that at Honolulu he said goodbye to the *Casco* and to Captain Otis, and on a bright June day in 1889 embarked on a trading schooner *The Equator*. She was commanded by an affable Scot, Captain Dennis Reid, experienced in trading in copra, and Stevenson soon made friends with him. *The Equator* was bound for the Gilbert Islands, a group of atolls in the Western Pacific, horseshoe-shaped and laced by lagoons of palms. The people of these islands were Micronesians, less attractive than the Polynesians, and differing in race and language.

Both Louis and Fanny were faced with problems, for the marriage between Belle and Joe Strong was not working out well. Fanny had never approved of her daughter's elopement with Joe and deplored their extravagance. He was a gifted artist, and according to Fanny "refined, artistic, affectionate, as weak as water, living in vague dreams". It was good of Louis to pay the Strongs' debts in Honolulu, and he not only supported his stepdaughter and husband financially, but was responsible for the education of their little son Austin. Belle and Louis clashed, and she was sent to Sydney, while Joe accompanied Louis, Fanny and Lloyd as cameraman on *The Equator*. Louis relates that he wanted to send Lloyd to Cambridge, but knowing that his stepfather was saddled with onerous financial responsibilities he decided not to go. In his early life Lloyd was far too dependent on Louis.

Louis noted the customs of the two chief places in the Gilberts, Bataritari and Apemana. There were marked changes. Women no longer went unclothed till marriage, and the widow no longer slept at night and sallied abroad by day with the skull of her dead husband. His first island in the South Seas had been the Marquesas, so different from the Gilberts. "The first experience can never be repeated," wrote Louis, the first love, the first sunrise, the first South Sea island are memories apart and touched a virginity of sense.[6] For him it was a love affair lasting the rest of his life.

Far the best part of *In the South Seas* is his portrait of the native King Tembinoka.[7] Stevenson described him as

> the one great personage in the Gilberts, the hero of song,
> the butt of gossip ... the last tyrant.... His corpulence is
> now portable, you would call him lusty rather than fat,

146

but his gait is still dull, stumbling and elephantine ... a beaked profile like Dante's in the mask, a mane of long black hair, the eye brilliant, imperious and inquiring ... his face was a fortune. His voice matched it well, being shrill, powerful and uncanny with a note like a sea-bird's. He was a greedy collector of clocks, musical boxes, blue spectacles and umbrellas, possessed by the seven devils of the collector.

Before allowing Stevenson to stay on his island, Tembinoka subjected the author to an ordeal, fixing upon him a hard and thoughtful stare, and finally telling him: "I look your eye. You good man. You no lie." Tembinoka could read character as well by the mouth. Louis told Colvin that despite his tyranny Tembinoka was very much a gentleman, a poet, musician, a historian, "or perhaps rather more a genealogist". He would lie in his house among a lot of wives writing *The History of Apemana* in an account book. He told Stevenson all kinds of strange stories for his South Seas book.

Whilst staying on Apemana, Fanny tended a garden of salad and shallots, although according to Louis, the salad was devoured by their hen. Food indeed presented a problem, for Apemana had little fish; however, Tembinoka occasionally presented them with a turtle and fish. Ah Fu, their Chinese cook, would shoot wild chicken in the bush and plover along the shore. The adventurers suffered much from a plague of flies and mosquitoes. A weird scene by lamplight and by mellow moonshine as a night-bird flew low over the trees with its hoarse croaking cry. According to Fanny,[8] King Tembinoka was very sad when he eventually said farewell. He remarked very pathetically, "I think you never saw a King cry before" and Fanny and Louis, too, shed tears. While Louis was on Apemana, Captain Reid on his trading expedition on *The Equator* had been unavoidably detained. So, the Stevensons were compelled to stay two months, instead of three weeks. At last the sails of their ship were sighted and to celebrate it there was a display of fireworks.

It was in Apemana that Stevenson, sometimes homesick for Scotland wrote these nostalgic verses:[9]

> The tropics vanish, and meseems that I
> From Halkerside, from topmost Allemuir
> Or steep Caerketton, dreaming gaze again.
> Far set in fields and woods, the town I see
> Spring gallant from the shallows of her smoke,
> Cragged, spired and turreted, her virgin fort
> Beflagged.

Louis also made a start on *The Wrecker*, a work of collaboration with Lloyd Osbourne, and losing some cohesion because of this. The plot was devised during moonlit conferences between Louis and his stepson on *The Equator*, and almost certainly inspired by the South Pacific. He is at his best in his descriptions of mighty storms at sea, and his ship's captain, Nares, might well be Captain Otis of the *Casco*. Overhead, the wild huntsman of the storm passed continuously, in one blare of mingled noises, screaming wind, straining timber, lashing rope's end, pounding block, and bursting sea contributed; and I could have thought there was at times another, a more piercing and more human note, that dominated all, like the wailing of an angel.[10] The early part of the book is set in Paris, and Louis could make full use of his memories of Fontainebleau in his description of the artists' life at Barbizon. To write a book is a very lonely task, and to collaborate with another person immensely difficult. It is impossible to say how much Lloyd contributed to the writing of *The Wrecker*, but the best parts reveal Stevenson's style. According to Fanny, some chapters were later completed in Apia, in Samoa, in the house of Harry Moors, the American trader, mostly on his verandah to the roar of the sea. It was sold to *Scribners* for serialization in 1891-1892.

On December 2nd when *The Equator* was 190 miles off Samoa, contending with prodigiously heavy seas, squalls, and rain mingled with calm spells, Louis wrote a detailed account to Colvin of his *South Seas* book. He usually referred to the British Museum where Colvin lived much of the time as "that gaunt old monument in Bloomsbury". It meant home for Louis, though he occasionally had passing thoughts of his rooms at Skerryvore, and the blackbirds in the Chine on a May morning. A lovely peaceful spot even today, the house destroyed by a German bomb, but the garden and its plaque are still there, Bournemouth's memorial to the valiant author.

By this time, Colvin and most of Louis's friends were heartily sick of Louis's panegyrics on the South Seas. Only Henry James, the most understanding of his friends, bore with him, though he missed him dreadfully.

When he first arrived in Samoa, Louis and Fanny had no thought during December 1889 of settling there. That came later. The Samoans - called by Europeans 'the Navigators' in earlier times - are a group of fourteen islands. The largest Savaii, is lava-strewn and in Stevenson's day barely inhabited.[11] Louis stayed in Apia, the capital of Upolu, important because of its foreign commerce for many centuries. We must imagine these islands surrounded by mountains and forests and bound by coral reefs. Louis told Baxter on December 29th that he thought Samoa far less beautiful than the Marquesas or Tahiti. "A more gentle scene, gentler activities, a tamer face of nature." The beautiful rivers reminded him of the Waters of Lothian. Louis always delighted in the sound of water. "Once I thought I was passing near a mill, and it was only the voice of the river." He was not at first especially attracted by the people, but the women were very handsome with lovely dresses, and the men lean, purposeful and dignified.

As Louis, Fanny, Lloyd and Joe Strong landed on Apia, they presented such a shabby appearance that the Rev. W.E. Clarke of the London Missionary Society, afterwards Louis's best friend in the islands, mistook them for impecunious entertainers. Fanny wore a large straw native hat and carried her guitar, Lloyd, short-sighted, wore dark glasses and carried a ukelele, and both Louis and Joe were dressed in their eccentric fashion.[12]

Louis and Fanny deliberated much before finally deciding to settle in Samoa. There were practical reasons. The communications at Samoa were excellent, for there were regular mail steamers, Sydney to Auckland and San Francisco. Postal communications were also promising. Louis now heard about the beneficial climate, a few hundred feet up in the mountains, cool with a balmy wind. If he was not on the sea, he liked to be in the mountains.

It was, however, the Michigan-born trader Harry J. Moors, who arranged that the Stevensons should rent a small cottage. It was largely owing to his advice and persuasion that they settled on the islands. "He was no petty swindler of savages on a remote island," wrote J.C. Furnas,

but owner of a chain of outlying trading posts and, per-
force, banker, factor, import agent, and local politician.
No mouse squeaked or plot hatched without his getting
some inkling.[13]

Whilst at sea, Louis would sometimes think of himself as a landed
proprietor and planter, and in this notion he would have been encouraged by Fanny, always keen on horticulture.

In his letter to his friend of Bournemouth days, Lady Taylor,
Louis first mentions the purchase of an estate - later called Vailima -
"Upon Upolu, some two or three miles behind and above Apia;
three streams, two waterfalls." Sir Percy Shelley had recently died
and Louis wrote of him to Lady Taylor: "He had a sweet, original
nature; I think I liked him better than ever I should have liked his
father." To Dr. Scott, his kind physician at Bournemouth, to
whom he dedicated *Underwoods*, his volume of poems, Louis wrote
on January 20th, 1890, of his vastly improved health.

I think nothing of long walks and rides. I was four hours
and a half gone the other day, partly riding, partly climbing up a steep ravine.[14]

Louis bought 314½ acres of what he described as "beautiful land
in the bush behind Apia", as he informed Baxter, travelling on a
German boat, the *Lubeck*, between Apia and Sydney. As so often
happened to Stevenson, his mind turned to the Edinburgh of his
youth and he enclosed some verses:

Do you remember - can we e'er forget?
How, in the coiled perplexities of youth,
In our wild climate, in our scowling town,
We gloomed and shivered, sorrowed, sobbed
                            and feared?
The rare and welcome silence of the snows,
The laggard morn, the haggard day, the night,
The grimy spell of the nocturnal town.
Do you remember? Ah, could one forget.

When Louis and Fanny arrived in Sydney, Belle and Austin were there to greet them. Because of their shabby appearance, however, they were refused admittance at a fashionable hotel, much to their annoyance. They were obliged to seek accommodation at another hotel, but the receptionist, who had behaved so discourteously, was much abashed when the hotel had to send on fan-mail to Louis. Journalists clamoured for interviews. He moved to the Union Club, but the Sydney climate never suited him, and he soon fell seriously ill, with fever, cough, pleurisy and even a severe haemorrhage. On March 7th 1890 he wrote Baxter that he "was a blooming prisoner here in the club, and indeed in my bedroom". He was certain that he would never return home except to die.

It was Fanny who probably saved his life, by arranging transport in a small steamer, *The Janet Nichol*. The ship was owned by a minor trading firm, Henderson and Macfarlane. They were at sea, from April to August, and Louis's health improved enormously. They visited many islands, including Apemana, where they saw King Tembinoka once again. During one gale at sea, Louis wrote Colvin, "I worked four to six hours per diem, spearing the ink-bottle like a flying fish, and holding my papers together as I might." In August he returned to Sydney, travelling by way of New Caledonia, where he dined with the French governor. Stevenson's queer encounters with Jack Buckland, a spendthrift for short periods in Sydney, and for the rest of the year a small trader in the islands, gave him the idea of a fictional character Tommy Hadden in *The Wrecker*, an amateur copra merchant in the South Seas and living an impecunious life in hansom cabs in Sydney. On rejoining Fanny during August in Sydney, Louis succumbed to illness again.

On recovery he was faced by a desperate quandary as to whether to return to England, for he longed to see his friends, especially Colvin, Baxter and James, or to stay permanently in the South Seas. To Henry James, far more understanding than Colvin, Louis confided: "I do not think I shall come to England more than once, and then it'll be to die." He only enjoyed good health in the tropics. When the thermometer in Sydney fell to almost 50° degrees, Stevenson knew that he could not stand the climate.

Stevenson and James, in their correspondence, frequently mention the rising star in literary England - young Rudyard Kipling. "Kipling is too clever to live" wrote Stevenson.[15] Both admired Kipling's genius, particularly as story-teller, but they were suspicious and had reservations. James wrote: "The talent enormous, but the brutality even deeper-seated",[16] while Stevenson wrote: "He alarms me by his copiousness and haste." In another letter:

> He is all smart journalism and cleverness; it is all bright and shallow and limpid. No blot of heart's blood, no harmony in the music.[17]

Stevenson later invited Kipling to Samoa, but the visit never materialized.

Edmund Gosse was patronizing and critical about Stevenson's work in the South Seas. He wrote to a correspondent:

> What do you think of Stevenson's *Ballads*. I confess we are all disappointed. The effort to become a Polynesian Walter Scott is a little too obvious, the inspiration too mechanical. There has been a great deal of disappointment among the few who have read the approaching *South Sea Letters*. The fact seems to be that it is very nice to live in Samoa, but not healthy to write there. Within a three-mile radius of Charing Cross is the literary atmosphere I suspect.[18]

That opinion might well have been shared by Colvin, but he never liked Louis so far away. In a rare letter to Fanny he unjustly criticized her for influencing Louis in his decision to remain in the South Seas. Aware of Louis's precarious health, it is difficult to excuse Colvin, though he naturally longed to see Louis in England. He, too, thought his work was deteriorating in the South Seas. Both Louis and Fanny were deeply hurt. He explained the situation very clearly to Frances Sitwell in a letter.

In the South Seas, I have health, strength. I can walk and ride and be out of doors, and do my work without distress. There are great temptations, on the other hand, to go home. I do not say it is to die - because I seem incapable of dying, but I know it is to go back to the old business.[19]

Louis and Fanny left Sydney in September, and a month later they were installed in a small cottage, where they were temporarily to live until a large house named Vailima - "five streams" - could be built. Meanwhile Lloyd was in England to arrange his stepfather's business affairs and to transport furniture from Skerryvore intended for the large house. Belle was soon to separate, at least temporarily, from Joe, a weak, hopelessly extravagant man, addicted to drink, and she too, was later to join the Stevenson clan at Vailima during May 1891. Louis, now, slowly resigned himself to his life, though he always remained an exile at heart, and increasingly nostalgic for his native Scotland.

XV

'The Buccaneering Pompadour of the Deep'

Henry James wrote to Stevenson from 34 de Vere Gardens on April 25th 1890, "You are indeed the male Cleopatra or Pompadour of the Deep - the wandering wanton of the Pacific." Stevenson always remained at heart the sea-rover, even when settled in Vailima.

Among his early acquaintances, visitors to Samoa, were the American historian Henry Adams and his artist friend, John La Farge. Louis was in his pioneer stage, attempting to make a home out of the dense forest in the hills above Apia, so it is hardly fair for Adams to be so critical and indeed uncharitable about the squalor of the Stevensons' dwelling. In a letter to Elizabeth Cameron he is, however, slightly ashamed, for he writes: "I must say no more in ridicule, for he has been extremely obliging, and given me very valuable letters of introduction to Tahiti and the Marquesas."[1] They dined with Adams and he relates "presently Mrs. Stevenson in a reddish cotton nightgown, staggered up the stairs and sank into a chair." He gives a vivid, brilliant picture of Louis

> dancing about, brandishing his long arms above his head and looking so attenuated in the thin flannel shirt which is constant wear. His sufferings here as a farmer are his latest fund for humour, and he described with bounds of gesticulation how he had just bought two huge farm horses and stabled them in a native house near his; and how at midnight, in a deluge and a gale of wind he had heard unearthly howls from the stable and had ventured out with a lantern. As he approached by the glimmer of the light, he became aware of two phantom excrescences protruding from the stable roof. These were his horses' heads.[2]

Henry Adams wrote to his correspondent that both La Farge and he came round to a sort of liking for Mrs. Stevenson, who was more human than her husband.

> His fragility passes description, but his endurance passes his fragility. I cannot conceive how such a bundle of bones unable to work on his writing without often taking to his bed as his working place should have gone through the months of exposure, confinement and bad nourishment which he has enjoyed.

Fanny's later complete breakdown in health is foreshadowed in Adams' references to her rheumatism and paralysis and illness of a dyspeptic nature. According to him, Stevenson gloated over discomforts and thinks that every traveller should sail for months in small cutters rancid with coconut oil and mouldy with constant rain and should live on coral atolls with nothing but coconuts and poisonous fish to eat. Adams compares the oriental delicacy of La Farge favourably with the Scottish eccentricities and barbarisms of Stevenson, who is as one-sided as a crab, and flies off at angles, no matter what rocks stand in his way.[3] One cannot rid oneself of an impression that Adams resented Stevenson's fame.

Louis refers to his acquaintances in a letter to Henry James (December 29th 1890):

> We have had enlightened society: La Farge the painter and your friend Henry Adams. We have almost nothing to eat; a guest would simply break the bank; my wife and I have dined on one avocado pear; I have several times dined on hard bread and onions.

If Adams had returned to Samoa, he would have formed a very different impression of Louis's generous hospitality in the splendour of Vailima.

Belle, his stepdaughter, was still in Sydney, but an absurd rumour spread about this time that she was Louis's daughter by a former non-Caucasian wife. She was now aged thirty-one, dark and very pretty.

Her mother was deeply hurt when Louis tactlessly said one day, towards the end of October 1890, that she had the true peasant nature and that she lacked the soul of an artist because she took such pleasure in the mere ownership of the land she was digging. "Had I the soul of an artist, the stupidity of possessions would have no power over me."[4] Fanny was, however, sometimes querulous, revealing a somewhat morbid mentality. He told her that her advice on artistic matters such as a book on the South Seas must be received with caution. His criticism rankled with his wife.

Meanwhile they both worked like beavers, Louis hacking away at the undergrowth and getting badly stung. One can read about his "long, silent contests" in the forest in *The Vailima Letters*.[5] Fanny also worked extremely hard in clearing paths in her future garden. Louis's toil seemed to benefit his health rather than to harm it. He proudly relates his struggles, assisted by many workmen, in 'The Woodman', one of the *Songs of Travel*:

> Thick around me in the teeming mud
> Briar and fern strove to the blood
> The hooked liana in his gin
> Noosed his reluctant neighbours in
> There the green murderer throve and spread
> Upon his smothering victims fed,
> And wantoned on his climbing coil.

People who think of the South Seas as eternal bliss, with an indolent sea lapping its sunlit shores are disillusioned when they peruse *The Vailima Letters*. For instance, Louis's letter (Christmas Eve, 1890):

> My wife near crazy with ear-ache; the rain descending in white crystal rods and playing hell's tattoo, like a *tutti* of battering rams on our sheet-iron roof; the wind passing high overhead with a strange dumb mutter, or striking us full, so that all the huge trees in the paddock cried aloud, and wrung their hands and brandished their vast arms.

They had, however, plenty of fun with a black sow they owned, named Jack Sheppard, and Louis's brown horse, Jack, gave him much amusement, though the German consul Dr. Stuebel said "O what a wild horse! It cannot be safe to ride him." Louis often rode on him to Apia.

Louis was working hard at his writing, finishing *The Wrecker* and planning a new book, provisionally called *The Pearl Fishers*, but renamed on publication *The Ebb-Tide*. Stevenson's methods, when embarking on his imaginative work described in a letter to a Glasgow correspondent, are of considerable interest - "I am still a slow study," he wrote,

> and sit for a long while on my eggs. Unconscious thought, there is the only method. Macerate your subject, let it boil slow, then take the lid off, and look in - and there your stuff is - good or bad.

Characteristic of his work was his serendipity, the faculty of making happy and unexpected discoveries by accident. Such was his story of the French prisoner of war, St. Ives.

In their small house, the Stevensons were much troubled by mosquitoes, and slow progress was being made on the building of the new house, to be finished by the middle of 1891. Fanny took infinite pains in its decoration, describing in her diary:

> The dining-room we have hung with a yellowish terra-cotta tapa, the window casings and door being a strong peacock blue, and the ceiling a sort of cream colour.... At the double window I have put a curtain of Indian gauze, cream-white and silver, lined with soft orange-coloured silk and edged with lace. My own room is beginning to have the softly jewelled look that I am so fond of.... The ceilings and walls are natural California redwood varnished.... The furniture is old mahogany with a little brass.... The window and door casings are a dark peacock green.[6]

Belle Strong related her vivid impressions of Samoa when she and her husband Joe and Austin her son rejoined her mother and stepfather during May 1891. "The perfumed air, the warmth, the flowering trees, and coco-nut palms enchanted her."[7] Louis called the Samoans "God's best, His sweetest work" and he did not exaggerate. An inseparable companion was Belle's tame cockatoo perched on her shoulder. She was delighted with her first glimpse of Vailima:

> Beyond a wide sweep of lawn rose a two-storey house with verandahs upstairs and down. Painted blue, with a red roof, it made a bright splash of colour.

Belle and Joe stayed in Pineapple Cottage where Fanny and Louis had lived before moving to the big house. Belle had loved her father Samuel Osbourne, but she had lost her early hostility for Louis and became attached to him. Misunderstandings were cleared away and Louis grew fond of Belle.

Everybody worked at Vailima. Louis rose at dawn to write, and breakfast was at six. At seven Lloyd and Joe made for the forest where they superintended Samoan workmen planting cocoa. Fanny was busy in her vegetable garden, planting innumerable seeds. Only once, during those last few years, did she leave Louis to go to Fiji for her health's sake. His mother, generally known as "Aunt Maggie", with her widow's cap, had now returned to Vailima, teaching Austin to recite reams of poetry from Burns, Byron, Sir Walter Scott, Shelley and Keats. Lloyd was very clever in finding a handsome Samoan named Talolo, at first completely inexperienced, but soon proving an excellent cook. Louis was delighted because he could now give lunch parties. Another invaluable addition to the household was Sosimo, a Samoan aged twenty. Belle trained him as a house-boy, but he soon grew attached to Louis, devoting himself to his service and acting as his valet. He looked after Louis's horse, Jack, and refused to allow anybody else to care for Jack. On one occasion when Talolo was away, Sosimo entered his master's room not only with Louis's tea, but also bringing an excellent omelette and a plate of buttered toast. Louis asked him, "Who did this?" speaking in Samoan. "I did," said Sosimo. "Great is your wisdom." "No," said Sosimo, "Great is my love."[8]

Belle managed the household, looked after their welfare and was very popular. The Samoans called her *Teuila*, adorner of the ugly, because she sometimes impulsively made the staff gifts of trinkets and scraps of cloth. Fanny's nickname was *Aolele*, flying cloud, for her perpetual skirmishing bustle, while Louis was always *Tusitala*, teller of tales. Furnas, however, wrote that there is some doubt whether *Tusitala*[9] was used specially to identify Louis, the first professional writer known to Samoans. *Tala* in Samoan means an elaborate rumour as well as a story. Today natives call any professional writer *Tusitala*.

One story written by Stevenson especially for the Samoans is *The Bottle Imp*,[10] really a fairy story related with a beautiful simplicity. It concerns the successive purchases and sales of a magic bottle, the conditions of purchase being made at a figure lower than the purchase. The certainty of hell is the fate of a person in his retention of the bottle until death. *Providence and the Guitar* is an entertaining story about the misadventures of some travelling musicians, but it does not draw its inspiration from the Pacific, rather from some encounters with some strolling players Louis experienced, during his stay at Grez-sur-Loing, when they performed at the Chevillon Inn. It was typical of Louis to send the cheque he received on publication, to the players.

As Louis was keenly interested in the political problems confronting Samoa at the period he resided there, it is necessary to sketch briefly their background. For many years there had been rivalry and animosity between the United States, Germany and Great Britain, but an attempt to settle these problems had been made at the Convention of Washington in 1878 and when it was reconvened at Berlin two years later. There were three rival native chiefs as potential kings of Samoa, Tarnasese, Laupepa and Mataafa. The Germans had at first deported Laupepa to Europe and elsewhere, but later had him reinstated as King. Mataafa much more popular than Laupepa, and possessing more ability, at first remained on amicable terms with Laupepa, but eventually became discontented because he was not given an influential position in the government. Withdrawing to a camp within a few miles of Apia, the capital, he maintained a semi-royal state as a focus of latent rebellion. Stevenson became attached to Mataafa and wrote during May 1892, "he is a beautiful, sweet old fellow".

Louis was always a Jacobite at heart and his eager sympathies always favoured Mataafa, whose character he admired. He attempted, however, to intercede between Laupepa and his main rival. In Louis's opinion the Chief Justice, a Swede, and the President, a German, were incompetent, and he used his influence in an attempt to get these officials withdrawn from Samoa. He did not enjoy cordial relations with the various Consuls on the islands, with the exception of Sewell, the American Consul, and in order to voice his strongly-held views, he wrote letters to *The Times*. The publicity and what they conceived as Stevenson's unauthorized interference, so exasperated the Chief Justice and the President of the Council that they demanded his deportation.[11] At home, Louis, however, received the warm support of the Foreign Secretary, his fellow Scot, Lord Rosebery, an admirer of *Treasure Island*, against the complaints of the British Consul.

Despite his involvement in Samoan affairs, and his ardent love for its natives, Louis always felt an exile. More and more his imagination turned to his beloved Scotland. During October 1891, Stevenson wrote to Henry James announcing *David Balfour* (later named *Catriona* on publication), the second part of *Kidnapped* "is on the stocks at last, and is not bad, I think." It was finished during the following year, and first published serially in *Atalanta* (1892-93) and given the title *David Balfour*, which has remained the American title. In his dedication to Charles Baxter, who often acted as his tough agent in Scotland, Louis wrote:

> You are still - as first I saw, as when I last addressed you - in the venerable city which I must always think of as my home. And I have come so far, and the sights and thoughts of my youth pursue me, and I see like a vision the youth of my father, and of his father, and the whole stream of lives flowing down there far in the north, with the sound of laughter and tears, to cast me out in the end, as by a sudden freshet, on these ultimate islands. And I admire and bow my head before the romance of destiny.

Stevenson might declare that he would never do a better book, but *Catriona* lacks the vitality of *Kidnapped*. Of his female characters, Barbara Grant is more satisfying than Catriona Drummond, the heroine of the story. The best portion of the book is the early part, but David Balfour's peculiar brother-and-sister relationship with Catriona when he takes her to Holland is hardly convincing. Again, there is a fatal reticence in a fully realized love story, as if Louis were held back by an unseen hand. Was it Fanny consciously or unconsciously influencing her husband, so that he could not as yet give full rein to his emotions? Frances Sitwell liked *Catriona*, but she told him, with insight, he would write a greater book.

Most of Louis's biographers have commented on his tendency to embark on two or three books at the same time. As he, himself, confessed, he was apt to tire of his characters in a longer work. Perhaps he lacked the physical endurance, hardly surprising when one considers his frail health, for continuous imaginative effort. He was certainly a far more natural writer of short-stories than a novelist, and found the former easier.

The best of his South Seas tales, however, *The Beach of Falesá*, showed that Stevenson was capable of great work. We find him writing to James Barrie, on November 1st 1892, a fellow Scot with whom he corresponded fairly frequently, but never knew:

> I have just finished *David Balfour*. I have another book on the stocks, *The Young Chevalier* (neither completed nor published) which is to be part in France and part in Scotland and to deal with Prince Charlie about the year 1749.

He mentions also that he had begun a third book about the immortal Braxfield, a legal luminary, who had always fascinated him. Another work *St. Ives* was never completed, and the reason for this may well have been the frustrating and difficult domestic problems with which he was contending during the last year or two of his life. They would no doubt have had a harmful effect on such a fine, creative writer and craftsman as Stevenson.

XVI
Friction at Vailima

Stevenson told Colvin (September 28th 1891) that he had written and rewritten *The Beach of Falesá*, something like sixty thousand words of sterling domestic fiction ... it is the first realistic South Sea story, the narrative of a South Sea trader, named Wiltshire, first published under the title *Uma*. She is a native woman, a female character, convincingly portrayed by Stevenson. *The Beach of Falesá* has the full flavour of the South Seas, more than *The Ebb-Tide*. One can smell the flowers and the trees of the village at night-time with the bread-fruit cooking. Its masterly beginning shapes Wiltshire's entire story.

> I saw that island first when it was neither night nor morning. The moon was to the west, setting, but still broad and bright. To the east, and right amidships of the dawn, which was all pink, the day-star sparkled like a diamond. The land breeze blew in our faces, and smelt strong of wild lime and vanilla.

Heady with a strange wanton beauty, like rare, exquisite wine. It is exciting, too, full of suspense, in the deadly rivalry of Wiltshire with the evil Trader Case, and the scene when Case is killed.

Colvin did not care either for *The Beach of Falesá*[1] or *The Ebb-Tide*, disliking seamy characters. Henry James, however, wrote to Louis:

> The art of *The Beach of Falesá*, seems to me an art brought to a perfection and I delight in the observed truth, the modesty of nature of the narrator.

162

With his sensitive perception he knew how difficult it was for his friend to reconcile the art of the novelist with the duties of an owner of a vast estate. Stevenson wanted to include *The Waif-Woman* as the fourth story of *The Island-Nights Entertainment*, but Fanny objected to it. Malcolm Elwes, in his book *The Strange Case of Robert Louis Stevenson*[2] speculates as to her objection, for it is a moral tale of a wife's possessive avarice punished by fate. It was only published after her death in 1914.

Louis wrote about *The Ebb-Tide*, a work which he began, in collaboration with Lloyd, in a denigratory way to Henry James:

> My dear man, the grimness of that story is not to be depicted in words. There are only four characters to be sure, but they are such a troop of swine! and their behaviour is really so deeply beneath any possible standard that in retrospect I wonder I have been able to endure them myself until the yarn was finished.

There are no female characters. Huish, the little cockney, is a vulgar, evil, depraved man, while Herrick, weak and unstable, is neither ultimately good nor bad.

Domestic problems plagued Louis during his last two years. It may well be that worries about the behaviour of his stepson-in-law Joe Strong during 1892 and earlier, coupled with his anxiety about Fanny's health during April 1893, shortened his own life. Joe, always mercurial, and addicted to drink, was having an affair with a native Samoan girl. According to Fanny, who never liked him, he was caught robbing the cellar and store-room at night with false keys.[3] He then went round Apia uttering all sorts of slanders against Belle, so Fanny and Louis had Joe sued for divorce. There was no difficulty in obtaining one. Belle merely mentions the divorce, and that Joe left Samoa to marry some years later "a charming young woman" in San Francisco, who loved him dearly. Fanny wrote in her diary that she had an attack of angina, when Joe came up late at night to Vailima to ask forgiveness. Louis assumed further responsibilities, becoming sole guardian of Austin, Belle's son. He was sent to school in Monterey, California, and cared for by Fanny's younger sister, the warm-hearted Nellie. Lloyd, too, who spoke

Samoan, was behaving badly. This was natural enough, but it caused his mother some distress.

Fanny was going through a bad period, subject to hysteria and jealousy. No wife could have cared more deeply for her husband, and looked after him more devotedly. She had earlier saved his life when he had suffered his fits of haemorrhage, but now it would seem that the strain of life at Vailima was affecting her own health, though she had suffered one complete breakdown even before marrying Louis. What grated with her was the knowledge that her husband, with his restored health, did not depend on her so much, nor did he seek so often her literary advice. She longed to be a personality in her own right, and in her garden she felt a true creator.

> When I plant a seed or a root, I plant a bit of my heart with it.... But I do feel not so far removed from God when the tender leaves put forth.... My heart melts over a bed of young peas, and a blossom on my rose tree is like a poem written by my son.[4]

Fanny resented the visit of Lady Jersey, the wife of the governor of New South Wales to Samoa during August 1892, thinking that Louis paid the lady too much attention and monopolized too much of his time. Lady Jersey stayed with Bazett Haggard, the Land Commissioner, brother of Rider Haggard the famous novelist. Knowing that she possessed some influence, Louis took her and her family to visit the rebel chief Mataafa whose cause he supported. Mataafa was the rival to the German-supported Malietoa. Louis loved this sort of cloak and dagger adventure, fancying himself a Jacobite, and calling Lady Jersey his cousin Amelia Balfour, to disguise her true identity.[5]

He wrote glowingly of Lady J. "She is really an orator with a golden voice" to Colvin when she opened a girls' school.[6] Fanny, however, was critical. She described her as:

> Tall and leggy, awkward, with bold black eyes and sensual mouth; very selfish and greedy of admiration, a touch of vulgarity, courageous as a man, and reckless as a woman.

On Thursday April 5th 1893 there is an ominous note in Louis's diary: "Well, there's no disguise possible. Fanny is not well, and we are miserably anxious." Her illness may have been psychotic as Jenni Calder opines.[7] She was hypersensitive, subject to hallucinations and delusions of grandeur, and on several occasions, Louis and Belle were forced to hold her down in her bed. She may have been temporarily out of her mind. Both Colvin and Graham Balfour, a visitor to Vailima in 1892, who wrote the authorized biography of Stevenson, are reserved about Fanny's illness. She could at least temporarily no longer give her husband the support, sympathy and understanding he needed.

Yet, as Louis confided to his diary, she had extraordinary recuperative powers. On April 7th, he wrote:

> I am thankful to say the new medicine relieved her at once. A crape has been removed from the day for all of us. To make things better, the morning is ah! Such a morning as you have never seen; heaven upon earth for sweetness, freshness, depth upon depth of unimaginable colour, and a faraway murmur of the Pacific and the rich piping of a single bird.

They were all seedy except Lloyd and Fanny. Louis was himself nearly extinct, Belle utterly overworked with rotten toothache, the cook with a bad foot, and butler suffering from an injury to his leg. "Eh, what a faim'ly," he added humorously.

By April 16th Louis was writing that Fanny was distinctly better, and in late April,

> A general, steady advance, Fanny quite chipper and jolly-self on the rapid mend, and with my eye on *forests* that are to fall - and my finger on the axe, which wants stoning.

What a picture he gives of a heavenly Sunday in Vailima:

> The world all dead silence, save when, from far down below us in the woods, comes up the crepitation of the little wooden drum that beats to church. Scarce a leaf

stirs; only now and again a great cool gush of air that makes my paper fly, and is gone.

Louis was eager to intercede between the King of Samoa and the rebel leader Mataafa, but his overtures were refused.

Henry James likened Fanny in her later life to "an old grizzled lioness" and by 1893 she was fifty-three. Louis himself wrote of his wife: "A violent friend, a brimstone enemy, is always either loathed or slavishly adored; indifference is impossible." Loving her, he was not blind to her faults.

Belle in her book *Memories of Vailima*[8] relates how she acted as her stepfather's amanuensis, writing to his dictation at least two of his books from 1892 onwards. Louis arranged with Baxter, in Edinburgh, that she should be paid. Perhaps she fancied herself Stevenson's Boswell, recording, whenever possible, his conversation. She certainly throws much light on his character. They had never been close until now, but Fanny, with her hypersensitivity and jealousy of Belle, for mother and daughter occasionally clashed, resented Louis and Belle being closeted together for hours. Beneath the surface of the harmonious family life at Vailima were hidden tensions and suspicions, deeply troubling to Louis. As amanuensis, Louis found Belle invaluable, but considered her not at all clever, but good. She was a poor speller.

When Louis was dictating, from 1892 onwards, the story of Anne de St. Ives, the escaped French prisoner of war, he and Belle sometimes worked on it from eight o'clock in the morning until four in the afternoon. It was Louis's curious way, when interested, to act the parts of his characters, so in *St. Ives* he described the interview between the old lady and the drover, speaking in a high voice for her and a deep growl for him. Once, when writing *The Master of Ballantrae*, he had entered Fanny's room to look in the glass to describe a haughty, disagreeable expression on the Master's face, actually expecting to see him, instead of merely seeing his own reflection in the glass. *St. Ives* is an adventure story, set in the Napoleonic era, 1813, and it gave Stevenson the opportunity to describe scenes so dear to him, such as Edinburgh Castle, Princes Street, the summit of the Pentlands and Swanston itself. "The cottage was a little quaint place," he wrote, of many rough-cast gables and grey roofs. It had something the air of a rambling infinitesimal cathedral, the body of it rising in the midst two stories high, with a steep-pitched roof, and sending out upon all hands (as it were chapter-houses, chapels and transepts), one-storeyed and dwarfish projections.[9]

It is a love story, that of St. Ives, a French nobleman, for Flora Gilchrist, an Edinburgh girl, and there are memorable little portraits of the French Colonel and of Mr. Robbie, the eccentric lawyer.

When writing *St. Ives*, Stevenson was much handicapped because essential books of research sometimes took six months to reach Vailima. He confessed to Colvin in March 1894: "I have had to change the first half of it from top to bottom." In his first draft, he wrote that the French prisoners in Edinburgh Castle were unshaved and clothed anyhow, only to discover that "they were watched over like a female charity school, kept in a grotesque livery and shaved twice a week".[10] Louis's letters to his old friend were so full of native affairs, of little interest to Colvin that he mildly protested, goading Louis to reply:

> Dear Colvin, please remember that my life passes among my blacks or chocolates.... You must try to exercise a trifle of imagination, and put yourself, perhaps with an effort into some sort of sympathy with these people or how am I to write to you? I think you are truly a little too cockney with me.

The war, by July 1893, had started between the followers of Laupepa and Mataafa, rival chiefs. Louis, who had once longed to be a soldier, had his first taste of war, visiting the wounded in the Mission House in Apia, together with Fanny and Lloyd. He described the night of July 9th,[11] "fine and starry though pretty cold", his own excitement, gloomy, yet truculent, for he blamed the white authorities for mishandling the whole affair. Clarke (the Rev. W.E.), his best friend on Samoa "was there steady as a die".

A magnificent Samoan with a noble aquiline countenance, very dark like an Arab, shot through both lungs, lay dying sur-

rounded by seven people fondling his limbs, and another lay awaiting "the last enemy" in a gloomy stupor of pain, taking laudanum.
The war went badly for Mataafa, for he was compelled to flee.
Louis, passionately interested in Samoan affairs, was later very kind
to political prisoners, and many of them owed their freedom from
gaol to him. As for Mataafa and his most important chiefs, they
were exiled to the German-held Marshall Islands.

Deep in *St. Ives* during the late summer of 1893, Louis had
no high opinion of it, telling Colvin: "*St. Ives* is unintellectual and
except as an adventure novel, dull." Belle relates that Louis believed
his own gift lay in the grim and the terrible, stories such as *Markheim*
and *Thrawn Janet*. Earlier in January, Louis was ill with threaten-
ings of a haemorrhage, and not allowed to speak. "Oh, poor *Anne*"
(her name for *St. Ives*), wrote Belle.[12] He lay in bed in his blue
and white Japanese kimono, with a wide red sash, never pale, but
smiling bravely. Ever resilient, he was able to continue with *St. Ives*
"in the deaf and dumb alphabet". In such a way, he dictated fifteen
pages. Belle was by no means altogether suited to the life of a pioneer, for she, herself, admitted to two terrors, a deadly fear of horses,
and of thunderstorms, sometimes devastating in Samoa. Knowing
of her daughter's dislike of riding, Fanny thoughtfully gave her a
gentle, mild brown mare, Peggy. Yet Belle was no coward.

Mail day in Vailima was a great occasion. It was always brought up on horseback by Sosimo, Louis's personal servant, in a big,
waterproof bag. It was Louis's custom to handle the mail-bag himself. "Woe betide the person who tries to snatch a letter from the
pile," wrote Belle. Several anecdotes showing Sosimo's devotion to
Louis are told. Once, during his master's last summer, June 1894,
Louis was temporarily absent, on board the *Curaçao*, travelling
to the island of Manua. Sosimo never smiled once, but on Louis's
return to Apia was the first to sight the man-of-war and to greet
his master on the beach, holding Jack (Louis's horse). He even
managed his master a little. On one occasion, Belle came into his
room to find her stepfather and Sosimo sorting papers. "Did you
tell Sosimo to do this?" she asked. "No," said Louis, "*he* told me."

During the summer of 1892 there was a welcome, new visitor
to Vailima. This was Graham Balfour, a cousin of Louis's on his
mother's side. An attractive younger man, he was to become warm-

ly attached to Louis, and to become a general favourite in the Vailima household. Belle fell in love with him. A brilliant scholar, versatile and tactful, he was a huge success in Samoa, helping Fanny in her garden, playing chess and piquet with Louis, visiting native villages with Lloyd, and lending a sympathetic ear to Belle's house-keeping problems. Since the natives found it difficult to pronounce Graham, they nicknamed him "Palema", a name used by all the Stevenson clan. This tall, powerful, handsome, fair man originally intended to come for a mere month, but on the insistence of the whole family, he stayed for a year.

In October 1901, the scholarly Balfour published the official life of *R.L.S.*, an admirable book in many ways. It is fair to add, however, that Balfour was too personally involved with Louis's family to write an entirely satisfactory life. Out of loyalty to his dear and venerated friend, and his sentiments for Fanny, who lived until 1914, discretion was absolutely essential. Balfour must have been aware of the tensions at Vailima during the last two years of Louis's life, his bursts of temper, caused by strained domestic con-ditions, affecting his powers of concentration, so that several plans for books were eventually abandoned. Yet he remained necessarily and resolutely silent about these matters.

The editor of the *Pall Mall Magazine* asked Henley to review Balfour's book, and although he was ageing and ill when he wrote it, and reluctant to undertake the work, his review was "not only mercilessly cruel", as Henley's sympathetic biographer[13] calls it, but brutal and unfair. For Henley there were "the two Stevensons", and he could never forgive him for going to America in 1887. Hen-ley had loved the "old, riotous, intrepid, scornful 'Lewis' of the Edinburgh days", so he condemned Balfour's book. "This seraph in chocolate, this barley-sugar effigy of a real man." He could never forgive Stevenson for being more successful than himself, though Louis had generously praised Henley's new volume of poetry.[14] "I did not guess you were so great a magician," he wrote. Yet Hen-ley accused him of stinginess. "I learn of his nameless prodigalities - and recall some instances of conduct in another vein," he added bitterly. "Of his vanity," he wrote, "he could not be in the same room as a mirror, but he must invite its confidence every time he passed."[15] Henley in his bitterness wanted to savage Fanny, for he hated her and wanted to wound her in her love for her husband.

In his last years, Louis became ever more attached to Samoa. When addressing the Samoan chiefs he told them: "I have chosen the land to be my land, the people to be my people, to live and die with."[16] His *A Footnote to History* is concerned with South Sea politics, a remarkable work praised by Furnas for Stevenson's description of the hurricane, a great document of the sea.

Louis strongly opposed the German influence in Samoa, and favoured Mataafa being given a high position on the island. This actually occurred, five years after Stevenson's death, when Germany, after taking over Western Samoa, appointed Mataafa undisputed "King".

Stevenson was much criticized at home for his political activities. A Foreign Office official noted on the back of a despatch: "Mr. Stevenson would do better if he stuck to novel-writing and left politics alone."[17] The firm of Tauchnitz was fined and prosecuted for reprinting *A Footnote to History* in Germany, and a missionary nearly sued Stevenson for libel.

Louis's birthday was usually celebrated on November 13th, but his forty-third birthday was postponed till December 10th, because of indisposition. His household feasted royally. There were sixteen pigs roasted whole underground, three enormous fish (Lloyd called them whales), 400 pounds of salt beef and of pork, 200 heads of Taro, enormous bananas, various native delicacies and 800 pineapples.

When the *Curaçao* was in port, life was very gay. Louis, Lloyd and Belle went to the officers' ball on a July evening, Belle escorted by her son Austin, now returned to the islands. Louis remarked that the *Curaçao* had restored his faith in human nature. The following day, Louis, Lloyd and Belle rode in the German flower parade (the Blumen Corso).

When thirty-seven cases, containing Louis's and Fanny's furniture, arrived from Scotland, including their silver and glass, they gave a lavish dinner party for twenty. Vailima looked resplendent with the large hall brilliantly lit at night.

Fanny's birthday was celebrated on March 10th 1894, her last with her beloved husband. Louis had thoughtfully pinned some verses to the "Stormy Petrel" on her mosquito-netting. "She was ever perilous and precious," he told her, "like an ember from the fire or a gem from a volcano."

Louis worked steadily on *St. Ives* during March 1894, while rumours of war flew around. He dictated to Belle, to the rolling of drums and his woods filling with scouting-parties. On one occasion she timidly asked him, "Louis, have we a pistol or gun in the house that will shoot?" To which he replied cheerfully, "No, but we have friends on both sides."

He planned another novel of the South Seas, to be called *Sophia Scarlet*[18] containing three female characters, but he never progressed further than the first two chapters of a rough draft.

He did not forget his old nurse "Cummy", writing to her in early 1893 and reminding her of the past:

> Do you remember when you used to take me out of bed in the early morning to show me the hills of Fife, and quote to me,

> A' the hills are covered wi' snaw
> An' winter's noo come fairly.

There were delicious days at Vailima, and horrid ones, but even as Cummy's "laddie" gazed at the blue sea and the crimson hibiscus his heart was yearning for his native Scotland. When the strident rain lashed the forest, even bursting upon Louis's roof with a great roar, the sound was sweet to him, for he told Colvin, "All smells of the good wet earth with a kind of Highland touch."

XVII

Weir of Hermiston

Stevenson always wrote his best when dealing with his own country, its people and places that he had known intimately in his youth and what is even more important, felt in his blood. In that spirit, "intent on my own race and place" he wrote the most widely acclaimed of his books *Weir of Hermiston*, a magnificent achievement, though unfinished.

He knew well the debt he owed to his wife, "prodigal of counsel", who had cherished and sustained him for fourteen years, despite occasional storms and bouts of ill health. So it was entirely fitting he should dedicate the book to his wife in elegant verses that never fail to stir our imaginations or our emotions. She found the dedication pinned to her bed-curtains:

> I saw rain falling and the rainbow drawn
> On Lammermuir. Hearkening I heard again
> In my precipitous city beaten bells
> Winnow the keen sea wind. And here afar
> Intent on my own race and place I wrote.
>
> Take thou the writing: thine it is. For who
> Burnished the sword, blew on the drowsy coal,
> Held still the target higher, chary of praise
> And prodigal of counsel. Who but thou?
> So now in the end, if this the least be good
> If any deed be done, if any fire
> Burn in the imperfect page, the praise be thine.

Already by the beginning of December 1891, Stevenson was planning the novel, referring to it in a letter to Baxter as *The Justice-*

Clerk, its first title. "It is pretty Scotch," he told him while he was working on the novel;

> the grand premier is taken from Braxfield ... mind you I expect "The Justice-Clerk" to be my masterpiece. My Braxfield is already a thing of beauty and a joy for ever, and so far as he has gone, by far my best character.

Adam Weir, Lord Hermiston, was modelled on the notorious Scottish judge Lord Braxfield. Louis asked Baxter to send him *Cockburn's Memorials*, in which he gives a damning portrait of Braxfield, vivid, yet perhaps prejudiced and Whiggish. J.D. Scott in an article 'The Myth of Lord Braxfield'[1] says that Braxfield is a historical character, for Stevenson's story is set in 1813. He implies that the historical character differed in essence from Cockburn's portrait. He was a famous hanging judge, possessing "a cherished coarseness", according to Cockburn. He once said to a loquacious man on trial in his low grumbling blacksmith's voice: "Ye're a vera clever chiel, man, but ye wad be nane the waur o'a hanging", an anecdote taken from Lockhart's *Life of Scott*. Stevenson asked Baxter to send him Pitcairn's *Criminal Trials*.

He was first attracted to Robert McQueen, Lord Braxfield, when he visited the Scottish Academy in 1876 or 1877 and saw his portrait by Raeburn. "A peculiarly subtle expression haunts the lower part," he wrote, "sensual and incredulous, like that of a man tasting good Bordeaux with half a fancy it has been somewhat too long uncorked."[2] He was the last judge to employ the pure Scottish idiom.

To Henry James, Stevenson wrote that he had drafted three chapters of *The Justice-Clerk* "which ought to be a snorter and a blower". Louis was later to put it aside as was his wont and to continue it with renewed appetite in the early autumn (1894). The title was changed to *Weir of Hermiston*, a title Colvin rightly preferred. According to Henley, the name "Weir" had a special significance for Louis, being the name of a famous Edinburgh character Major Weir, a warlock, who was accused of incest with his sister and burnt at the stake.[3]

To a Scottish correspondent S.R. Crockett, a sincere admirer and an aspiring writer, Louis wrote during May 1893 that *Weir of Hermiston* was scarce begun. Glengorse Church in the Pentlands is described in Chapter VI, a place dear to Louis's heart. "I shall never take that walk by the Fisher's Tryst," he wrote Crockett.

> I shall never see Auld Reekie. I shall never set my foot again upon the heather. Here I am until I die and here will I be buried.

He thought that the plot was not good, but it was in fact excellent. Since Crockett had dedicated a book to Stevenson, in return, he sent him one of his best poems, full of the austere grandeur of the "wine-red" moors he so loved in his dreams of home.

> Blows the wind today, and the sun and wind are flying,
> Blows the wind on the moors today and now,
> Where about the graves of the martyrs the whaups are
> crying,
> My heart remembers how!
>
> Grey and recumbent tombs of the dead in desert places,
> Standing-stones on the vacant wine-red moor,
> Hills of sheep, and the howes of the silent vanished races,
> And winds, austere and pure:
>
> Be it granted me to behold you again in dying,
> Hills of home! and to hear again the call,
> Hear about the graves of the martyrs the peewees crying,
> And hear no more at all.[4]

Under the influence of that intrepid lady, his mother, Louis started a custom, familiar to every Samoan household, the holding of family prayers. One cannot imagine Louis in his prime, an agnostic, at 17 Heriot Row conceiving the idea. Fanny has described in her introduction to *Prayers Written at Vailima* how at eventide

174

when all work was over the 'pu' or war conch would sound. The white members of the household would take their customary places in the vast hall while the Samoans squatted on the floor beneath a large lamp that hung from the ceiling. Outside the savage, monotonous sound of native drums would almost drown the service.

Lloyd would start by reading a chapter from the Samoan bible while Maggie Stevenson sat wearing her black widow's dress and white cap, with Belle and Austin Strong beside her and any guests at Vailima. One such prayer reads:

> Grant that we here before Thee may be set free from the fear of vicissitude and the fear of death, may finish what remains before us of our course without dishonour to ourselves or hurt to others, and when the day comes, may die in peace.

Stevenson made friends wherever he went, and in Samoa he had intimate friends such as Rev. W.E. Clarke of the London Missionary Society and his wife. "A man I esteem and like to the soles of his boots. I prefer him to anyone in Samoa, and to most people in the world."[5] Another staunch friend of Louis's and Fanny's was the U.S. Consul Henry Ide, afterwards Chief Justice. When Louis discovered that Ide's daughter Annie's birthday was on Christmas Day, he charmingly signed a deed making a present of his own birthday. His friendship also prospered with Bazett Haggard, brother of Rider, author of *King Solomon's Mines*.

Edmund Gosse wrote to Louis: "Since Byron was in Greece, nothing has appealed to the ordinary literary man so much as that you should be living in the South Seas." Now, however, that he was famous, the romance of his life with its travels to exotic places had lent itself to all sorts of legends, injuring his literary reputation and obscuring what really mattered, his permanent importance as a writer.

During the last year of his life, Louis did some very hard thinking on his changed conception of sex. This is reflected in a long letter to his cousin Bob during September 1894. It smacked of depression.

But as I go on in life, day by day, I become more of a
bewildered child. I cannot get used to this world, to
procreation, to heredity, to sight, to hearing; the com-
monest things are a burthen.

He had always possessed a sense of open-mouthed wonder, finding
beauty in unexpected places. Perhaps he regretted that he had never
experienced the joy of fatherhood, but he had denied himself this,
knowing he could not have borne the responsibility of a possible
child inheriting his infirmities. When Henley became father to an
infant daughter, Louis had envied him, but children bring pain as
well as pleasure and her early death had shown him his error in
envying Henley.

Later in the same letter he wrote:

If I had to begin again - I know not - *si jeunesse savait,
vieillesse pouvait* - I know not at all - I believe I should
try to honour sex more religiously. The worst of our
education is that Christianity does not recognize and
hallow sex. It looks askance at it, over its shoulder,
oppressed as it is by reminiscences of hermits and Asiatic
self-torturers. It is a terrible hiatus in our modern religions that they cannot see and make venerable that which
they ought to see first and hallow most.[6]

Louis was freed at last. The myth of Lord Braxfield enabled
him to free his talent. In *Hermiston* he could realize fully the dem-
oniac quality of the Scot's national character.[7] He could describe
sex in a natural way in his great work - the unfinished fragment
the *Weir of Hermiston*. The young Kirstie is gloriously alive, a
creature of passion, unlike Alison Durie in *The Master of Ballantrae*.
One can feel for her distress, her pining to be loved. There had
been misunderstandings between Archie and Christina. Here is part
of the last paragraph:

Archie ran to her. He took the poor child in his arms,
and she nestled to his breast as to a mother's and clasped
him in hands that were strong like vices. He felt her

176

whole body shaken by the throes of distress and had
pity upon her beyond speech.

Perhaps when writing these lines, Louis remembered his own need
in youth for a mother, mistress and wife all centred in one woman.
Writing at the height of his powers, these female characters are
magnificent portraits, the elder Kirstie especially, with her secret
hatred of Archie's father and her shrewdness and possessive love of
Archie Weir. "... a bonny figure o' a woman when a lassie, built to
rear bairns." The two best chapters are 'The Hanging of Duncan
Jopp' ending with the confrontation between Archie and the Judge,
his father, and the nocturnal meeting between Archie and the elder
Kirstie. Adam Weir is a brilliant creation, undeniably a great lawyer,
but coarse, partial to foul mirth and a mighty toper, like Lord
Braxfield.

Louis was much beloved in Samoa, especially by the native
chiefs, his friends. They felt eternally grateful to him for securing
their release from prison. To mark their gratitude, they offered to
build for him free, what he named "The Road of Gratitude", but
they preferred to call it "The Road of living hearts". Belle wrote
on August 27th 1894:

> We have worked at *Anne* (*St. Ives*) all these mornings
> when the guns were firing at Atua ... They were inter-
> rupted by the arrival of eight chief political prisoners, all
> expressing genuine gratitude for their release and record-
> ing with infinite affection all the kindnesses they had
> received from Louis. In proof of their gratitude they
> offered to make a road sixty feet wide connecting us
> with the highway across the island.[8]

Louis gave sage and passionate advice to the Samoan chiefs when
he addressed them in October. Indulging in civil warfare was dis-
astrous for their islands.

> There is but one way to defend Samoa.... It is to make
> roads and gardens, and care for your trees, and sell their
> produce wisely, and in one word, to occupy and use your
> country. If you do not others will.[9]

Writing on September 24th, Belle relates: "Louis and I have been writing, working away every morning like steam-engines on *Hermiston*." One might almost think she was part author of the work. He had tired of *St. Ives* and, as was his way when his inspiration flagged, turned aside from it, having achieved thirty chapters. Perhaps he was influenced by Lloyd, who had criticized one of the love-scenes when Louis had read the novel aloud. *St. Ives* was never completed. After Stevenson's death, his editor Sidney Colvin asked Conan Doyle to finish it, but it was Arthur Quiller-Couch, a Cornishman and don of Jesus College, Cambridge, who eventually undertook the task. The book was published in 1897. Since those times, new researches have been discovered by R.J. Storey, a diligent researcher, notably about the activities of American privateers off the west coast of Scotland and Jenni Calder, a distinguished biographer of Stevenson, has written a new version containing five chapters. The University of Cramond is supposed to be based on Stevenson's experiences in Edinburgh University, the last chapter he wrote.

Everything went well with *Hermiston*. "He has always been wonderfully clear and sustained in his diction," wrote Belle. "He walks up and down the room, as I write." His voice was so mellifluous and the story so gripping that she was enraptured. She was thrilled when her stepfather told her he had modelled young Kirstie on her, though it is difficult to find any real resemblance. No doubt Belle could suggest what his heroine might wear. In one chapter Christina wears a grey dress cut with short sleeves and skirts and her pink stockings and kerchief she wore round her shoulders were probably Belle's idea.[10]

It was a wonderful moment for a creative artist surveying his own work, and knowing intuitively it was good. "Belle, I see it so clearly," he said, "the story unfolds itself before me to the least detail - there is nothing left in doubt. I never felt so before in anything I ever wrote."

He was always hospitable, always ready to greet visitors, especially his native Scots. One day at the end of November, only three days before his death, three Scottish sailors from the *Wallaroo*, an American ship, came up to Vailima, "like homing pigeons", asking for a drink of water. Although he was deeply immersed in *Hermiston* and it was Thanksgiving Day when the cook was experimenting with some Samoan berries intended for cranberry sauce for a dinner party, Louis took them over the house. He showed them his treasures, his busts and statues, the large picture of Skerryvore lighthouse built by his grandfather and the specimen of Gordon of Khartoum's writing in Arabic letters on a cigarette paper. They were especially interested in a rare edition of Burns. One of the sailors, who lived in Edinburgh, was given Louis's book of poems, *Underwoods*, suitably inscribed. As they walked away, Louis said smiling, "How I love a blue-jacket! What a pity we can't invite them to our dinner tonight, they would be so entertaining."

One of his last letters was to Edmund Gosse, "his dear Weg", acknowledging the dedication "To Tusitala" (teller of tales) of his volumes of poems *In Russet and Silver*.

For a few days, Fanny, at the beginning of December, had been unable to rid her mind of forebodings that something terrible was about to happen to an intimate of the family. She did not connect her fears with Louis, but was convinced that Graham Balfour, then on the high seas, was facing unknown dangers. Louis was in high spirits, elated about *Hermiston*. One evening, he read the opening chapters to his family, but was greatly agitated when Lloyd merely murmured "Good night Louis". Mistaking his silence for lack of approval, Louis exclaimed, "My God, you shall not go like that. No note, no comment, not even the courtesy of a lie."[11]

In reality Lloyd had been deeply impressed by the work, convinced that it was a masterpiece, a great novel in the English language. In the silence, with the stars glowing brightly in the tropical sky, Louis, mollified, sat on the verandah with Lloyd talking about intimate matters, too sacred to be revealed. During those last weeks Lloyd had often seen Louis look a trifle wistfully up at the forest-clad Vaea mountain where he had asked to be buried.

On December 3rd Belle noticed how cheerful Louis was, dictating the last passages of his *Hermiston*. He was ardently looking forward to Baxter's visit to Vailima. Now a widower, for he had recently lost his wife Gracie, Baxter was on the way to Samoa, saddled with the first volume of the Edinburgh edition of his works. If Louis had lived, would he have been able to sustain to the end *Hermiston's* wonderful power? To me the grim story is a tragedy throughout, and to make it anything else is utterly false.

Stevenson had planned the subsequent action. Frank Innes, "the young fool advocate" seduces young Kirstie and makes her pregnant. She confesses part of the truth to Archie whom she loves, but does not name her seducer. Archie, suspecting the truth, then meets Frank Innes by the Weaver's Stone, forces an argument and shoots him dead. He is eventually tried for murder and condemned to death. It is the planned ending one quarrels with, the breaking of prison and the securing of his release by young Kirstie's brothers, the escape to America and the marriage with his beloved. No doubt a fascinating story, but if he really contemplated it, false to his artistic ideals.

Louis died in harness as he would have preferred. At sunset on the fatal day he read the last pages of his book to Fanny, for the most part his shrewd and able critic, and did his utmost to stir her from her despondent mood, suggesting a game of cards and talking gaily about going on a lecture tour of America. He went to the cellar to fetch a bottle of his favourite Burgundy, helping her to mix a dressing for the salad for their evening meal. They were walking on the verandah, Louis talking in his animated way when he suddenly put his hands to his head, exclaiming, "What's that? Do I look strange?" Fanny and the devoted Sosimo helped his Tusitala onto an easy chair, and Maggie and Belle came at Fanny's summons. Lloyd made a dramatic ride to Apia to fetch Dr. Funk and the surgeon of the *Wallaroo*. It was of no avail. Sosimo, a Catholic, asked that the Vailima Catholics should sing their own hymns over him, and watched all night beside his master, while the Reverend Clarke prayed beside the man he had so admired and loved. Louis died at eight o'clock in the evening, almost one hundred years ago, without regaining consciousness, aged forty-four and three weeks. Was Louis granted his prayer? "Be it granted to behold you again in dying, Hills of home." Perhaps in his dazed sleep of death he was vouchsafed his wish.

Then the last dramatic, eerie scene on the following day when Louis's body was carried up the steep mountain side to the top of Mount Vaea at 1 p.m. on the shoulders of forty sturdy Samoans. He was buried there and on the grave is a plaque containing his celebrated verses:

> Here he lies where he longed to be,
> Home is the sailor, home from the sea,
> And the hunter home from the hill.

Twenty years later when Fanny after long, weary, mixed years, mostly in California, was laid to rest next her husband, there is another plaque commemorating this brave woman:

> Teacher, tender comrade, wife
> A fellow-farer, true through life.

It was thoughtful of the Samoans, so respectful in their grief, to forbid the use of firearms in the mountains. Stevenson had always rejoiced in the songs of birds, whether in his native Scotland, in Mentone or in the South Seas. So, in the desolate silence they sang sweetly about his grave.

Epilogue

When Louis's friends in England first heard reports of his death, they could hardly credit them, but the grim truth soon spread. Colvin wrote to Gosse:

> To us who knew and loved him, half the light of our world has gone out. For himself it is strange how full several of his latest letters have been of the longing for an early death.[1]

Henry James, more emotional, visited Frances Sitwell, crying: "It isn't *true*, it isn't true, say it isn't true." To Edmund Gosse he wrote:

> Of what can we think or utter or dream, save of this ghastly extinction of the beloved R.L.S.? Today at any rate, it's a cruel wringing emotion. One feels how one cared for him - what a place he took, and as if suddenly into that place there had descended a great avalanche of ice. I'm not sure that it's not for *him* a great and happy fate, but for us the loss of charm, of suspense, of "fun" is unutterable.

He was desolate, although he declined to act as an executor. His message of condolence to Fanny was expressed in fine language and tactfully:

> What can I say to you that will not seem cruelly irrelevant or vain? We have been sitting in darkness for nearly a fortnight, but what is our darkness to the extinction

of your magnificent light. You are nearest to the pain, because you were nearest the joy and the pride.[2]

Stevenson was a writer of remarkable versatility, essayist, playwright, novelist, writer of fables, poet, writer of ballads, and travel writer, but he was greatest as a writer of short stories, at his best in this medium. *Thrawn Janet, The Beach of Falesá, Providence and the Guitar, The Merry Men, The Bottle Imp,* and *Treasure of Franchard* are first class stories and can be compared with those of Somerset Maugham - a more subtle analyst of character than Stevenson and Rudyard Kipling. As a letter writer Stevenson is always fascinating and often funny, and his correspondence reveals the man and writer more than anything else. Today - almost a hundred years since his death - his books are not widely read, except for *Treasure Island, Kidnapped, A Child's Garden of Verses* and possibly that graceful and charming *Travels with a Donkey in the Cévennes*. And of course, *The Strange Case of Dr. Jekyll and Mr. Hyde* is known throughout the civilized world.

Many people would be the richer if they were familiar with the essays in *Virginibus Puerisque*, such as 'Falling in Love' or 'An Apology for Idlers'. His own favourites were 'Child's Play' and 'Pan's Pipes'. 'Child's Play' is a delicate, intuitive understanding of a child's mind, and 'Pan's Pipes' is fanciful and full of poetic feeling. Perhaps if he had lived longer than 1894, he might have written another great saga of the South Seas, but his mind had returned to the scenes of Scotland while he worked feverishly on *Weir of Hermiston*. It is futile to conjecture what he might have achieved if granted longer life. Edwin Muir, a cautious critic, has no reservations about *Hermiston*. He wrote:

> He began when he was over forty to speak in the unaffected voice of the great writer.... We see in a flash all that he might have become ... a noble gentleness and flexibility. The figures exist in a clear dawn, and have the freshness of a morning race where everyone without effort or distortion is a little above the human scale. They differ from Hardy's characters, tragic in a lesser fashion, by their integral and active powers. Judging him by it, one can almost say that no other writer of his time showed evidence of equal powers.[3]

Notes

CHAPTER I

1. See an article by David Angus, *The Scot's Magazine*, August 1979.
2. I was recently entertained there by Lord and Lady Dunpark.
3. See pp. 83 et seq., 1904 edition, Chatto & Windus.
4. Coolin miti et blando, qui viridi senectute apud trivium ubi venatores convenire solent, casi quodam infelice diem suprenum obiit. Hune lapidem in memoriam posuerunt moerentes amici, 1869 R.L.S.
5. I am indebted to David Angus for bringing to my attention Margaret Stevenson's Diary.
6. Page 18, *Robert Louis Stevenson and His World*, David Daiches.
7. Ibid., *Robert Louis Stevenson and His World*.
8. Page 161, Pocket edition of *Kidnapped*, Cassell & Company.
9. See *The Life and Letters of Sir Edmund Gosse* by The Hon. Evan Charteris.
10. *R.L.S.: A Life Study*, Jenni Calder.
11. Published in *Memories and Portraits*.
12. Ibid., *Memories and Portraits*.
13. Ibid., *R.L.S.: A Life Study*
14. Mss National Library of Scotland, Mss 8790.

CHAPTER II

1. *Poems by Allan Ramsay and Robert Fergusson*, edited by Alexander Manson Kinghorn and Alexander Law.
2. May 18th, 1894. *The Letters of Robert Louis Stevenson*, Vol. IV.
3. *Voyage to Windward*, Furnas, 1952.
4. *Stevenson's Letters to Charles Baxter*, edited by De Lancey Ferguson, 1956.
5. Ibid. *R.L.S.: A Life Study*, Jenni Calder.
6. *The Life of Robert Louis Stevenson*, Rosaline Masson.
7. He inherited the title from his father.
8. The late fourteenth century religious reformer.
9. Ibid. *Stevenson's Letters to Charles Baxter*.
10. First published 1982. From the unfinished manuscript (from the Edwin Collection, Yale University Benecke mss.).
11. See *The Introduction to the Edifying Letters of the Rutherford Family*, pp. 19 & 20.
12. Ibid. *Introduction to the Edifying Letters of the Rutherford Family*, pp. 19 & 20.
13. Ibid. *Memories and Portraits*.

CHAPTER III

1. *R.L.S.: A Life Study*, Jenni Calder.
2. Louis later burnt her letters. Mrs. Sitwell was not married to Sidney Colvin until 1903.
3. Mss. 4383, fol. 99. National Library of Scotland.
4. Bertie died later in Switzerland, a great sadness for Mrs. Sitwell. Another of her sons had already died.
5. National Library of Scotland Mss. *R.L.S.: A Life Study*.
6. Mss. 8790, fol. 53. National Library of Scotland.
7. See *The Strange Case of Dr. Jekyll and Mr. Hyde*. Fables and other stories and fragments.
8. Selected English Classics: *Travels with a Donkey* and *Virginibus Puerisque*.
9. Mss. 90, fol. 88. National Library of Edinburgh.
10. Ibid. Mss. 90, fol. 101.
11. Ibid. Mss. 90, fol. 117.
12. This essay can be read in *Familiar Studies of Men and Books*.
13. Ibid. *The Life of Robert Louis Stevenson*, Rosaline Masson.
14. Ibid. *Familiar Studies of Men and Books*, p. 12.
15. The first edition actually published in December 1874, though first edition dated 1879.

CHAPTER IV

1. Robert L. Stevenson, James Pope Hennessy, 1974.
2. National Library of Scotland mss.
3. Born in 1849, so a year older than Stevenson.
4. *Chronicle of Friendships*, 1873-1900.
5. Ibid. *Chronicle of Friendships*.

CHAPTER V

1. *Life of Mrs. R.L. Stevenson*, Sanchez.
2. Ibid. Sanchez.
3. Ibid. *R.L.S.: A Life Study*, Jenni Calder.
4. Ibid. *Chronicle of Friendships*.
5. The Hôtellerie du Bas-Breau on the site where it is claimed R.L.S. wrote *Forest Notes*.
6. Lloyd Osbourne, Introduction, *New Arabian Nights*, 1852, I, p. viii.
7. Ibid. *Chronicle of Friendships*, p. 153.
8. This essay was later published in Henley's *Magazine of Art*.
9. Ibid. Pope Hennessy, *Robert L. Stevenson*, 1974.
10. Ibid. *R.L.S.: A Life Study*, Jenni Calder.
11. Belle became Mrs. Strong on her first marriage.
12. See Henley's review of Graham Balfour's *Biography of R.L.S.*, published December 1901, *Pall Mall Magazine*.

13. *A Study in the Counter Decadence of the Nineties*, J.H. Buckley, 1945.
14. Ibid. *Robert Louis Stevenson*, Pope Hennessy.
15. Ibid. National Library of Edinburgh, mss. 8790.
16. *The Strange Case of Robert Louis Stevenson*, Malcolm Elwin, p. 190.
17. *Caroline Norton* by Alice Acland, 1948.
18. Mss. 4366, fol. 139. National Library of Edinburgh.
19. Ibid. *Robert Louis Stevenson*, Pope Hennessy.

CHAPTER VI

1. Published in *Virginibus Puerisque*.
2. Illustrated Edition published by Rupert Hart Davis, p. 78, 1954.
3. The Club had moved to Piccadilly.
4. *Familiar Studies of Men and Books*, Chatto & Windus, 1905.
5. Ibid. *The Strange Case of Robert Louis Stevenson*, Malcolm Elwin.
6. Ibid. *The Life of Mrs. Robert Louis Stevenson*, Chatto & Windus.

CHAPTER VII

1. Prefatory note by Mrs. R.L. Stevenson, *The Amateur Emigrant* by Robert Louis Stevenson, 1924.
2. R.L. Stevenson, *The Amateur Emigrant: The Silverado Squatters*, Heinemann, p. 23.
3. *Across the Plains*, second part of *The Amateur Emigrant*.
4. Ibid. *Across the Plains*.
5. Ibid. *Life of Mrs. R.L. Stevenson*, Sanchez.
6. Ibid. *Robert Louis Stevenson and His World*, David Daiches, p. 41.
7. *A Child's Garden of Verses*, facsimile edition, 1990, p. 133.
8. Ibid. *Stevenson's Letters to Charles Baxter*, edited by Dr. Lancey Ferguson, 1956.
9. See Act V, Scene One, *Hamlet*, Shakespeare.
10. According to Nicholas Rankin in *Dead Man's Chest* it was saved from destruction by two ladies and given to the State of California, 1941.
11. *Collected Poems* edited by Janet Adam Smith.

CHAPTER VIII

1. Collected Letters.
2. *Underwoods*, Chatto & Windus, 1909.
3. Preface, *Lyrics*, Rich and Cowan, 1935.
4. 'Old and New Pacific Capitals', *The Amateur Emigrant*.
5. Ibid. Letters, edited by Sir Sidney Colvin, II. 77.
6. Joe Strong also designed the frontispiece to *The Silverado Squatters*.

CHAPTER IX

1. Ibid. *A Life Study*, Jenni Calder.
2. Ibid. R.L. Stevenson, Letters I. To his Family and Friends. Selected and edited by Sidney Colvin.
3. *Robert Louis Stevenson*, W.G. Lockett.
4. Ibid. *Familiar Studies of Men and Books*, Chatto & Windus.
5. See *Bacon's Essays*, Golden Treasury Series, p. 26.
6. Ibid. *The Letters of Robert Louis Stevenson to His Family and Friends*.
7. Ibid. *Underwoods*, Chatto & Windus, 1909, p. 58.
8. Hôtel du Pavillon Henri IV where Louis XIV was born 1638.
9. Stevenson to Colvin from Pitlochry, July 1881.
10. Ibid. *The Merry Men and Other Tales and Fables* (first published 1887) Chatto & Windus, 1907.
11. Ibid. *The Letters of Robert Louis Stevenson*, selected and edited by Sidney Colvin, Vol. I.
12. Ibid. *Life of Mrs. R.L. Stevenson*, Sanchez.
13. Page 120.
14. Ibid. Pope Hennessy, *Robert Louis Stevenson*, p. 154.
15. Ibid. *The Art of Writing*, p. 121.
16. *The Violent Friend*, MacKay; also *R.L.S.: A Life Study*, Calder.
17. Ibid. *Letters of R.L. Stevenson*.

CHAPTER X

1. Ibid. *Life of Mrs. R.L. Stevenson*.
2. Ibid. *The Merry Men and Other Tales and Fables*.
3. Ibid. *Life of Mrs. R.L. Stevenson*, Sanchez.
4. Ibid. *The Letters of Robert Louis Stevenson*.
5. Mentioned in Nicholas Rankin's *Dead Man's Chest*.
6. Ibid. *Letters of R.L. Stevenson*.
7. See *Telegraph Magazine*, August 4th, 1990. The Mss. of *The Enchantress* is now in the Bancroft Library of the University of California at Berkeley.
8. Ibid. *Letters of R.L. Stevenson*.
9. Ibid. *Life of Robert Louis Stevenson* by Sir Graham Balfour, I. 205.
10. Ibid. *The Strange Case of Robert Louis Stevenson*, p. 187.
11. Ibid. *Robert Louis Stevenson*, Letters I. 336.

CHAPTER XI

1. I have an old battered copy given me by my former tutor at Eton, Charles Gladstone, the G.O.M.'s grandson.
2. Published as last essay in *Memories and Portraits*.
3. Ibid. *Henry James and Louis Stevenson: A Record of Friendship and Criticism*, with an introduction, 1948.
4. Ibid. See XVII.
5. *R.L.S. and His Sine Qua Non*, 1929, by Adele Boodle.

6. Ibid. Page 76, Adele Boodle.
7. Ibid. *R.L.S. and His Sine Qua Non*, p. 118.
8. National Library of Edinburgh, MS.3786.
9. See Dedication in *Underwoods*, 1909, Chatto & Windus.
10. Ibid. *Robert Louis Stevenson*, Pope Hennessy.
11. Ibid. *Letters of Robert Louis Stevenson*, I. 362.
12. Ibid. *R.L.S.: A Life Study*, Jenni Calder.
13. *Kidnapped*, Cassell and Company.
14. Born in 1809, died in 1849, the year before Stevenson's birth.
15. See *Markheim* in *The Merry Men and Other Tales*, Chatto & Windus, 1907.
16. Karl Miller in *Cockburn's Millennium* has an interesting chapter on double lives, pp. 190-209.
17. See p. 61, *The Strange Case of Dr. Jekyll and Mr. Hyde*, William Heinemann.
18. Ibid. *Henry James and Robert Louis Stevenson: A Record of Friendship and Criticism*.
19. *Opium and the Romantic Imagination*, Alethea Hayter, 1968.
20. Ibid. *Opium and the Romantic Imagination*.
21. Ibid. *The Life and Letters of Sir Edmund Gosse* by The Hon. Evan Charteris, 1931.

CHAPTER XII

1. Ibid. *Life of Mrs. Robert Louis Stevenson*, Sanchez.
2. He had recently painted Louis's portrait at Skerryvore.
3. Ibid. Graham Balfour's Biography of Stevenson.
4. Ibid. *Letters of Robert Louis Stevenson*, Vol. III, 1887-1891.
5. Ibid. *Letters of Robert Louis Stevenson*, Vol. III, p. 19.
6. Ibid. *Letters of Robert Louis Stevenson*, Vol. III, p. 35.
7. Ibid. *Robert Louis Stevenson*, Pope Hennessy, p. 193.
8. Later included in 'The Art of Writing', Chatto & Windus, 1905.
9. Henley to R.L.S. See John Connell's biography *W.E. Henley*, Constable and Co.
10. Ibid. *Robert Louis Stevenson*, Pope Hennessy.
11. National Library of Scotland Advocates Library Mss. 26.81, fol. 4-6.
12. National Library of Edinburgh Mss. F2.17.
13. See Sidney Colvin's note to Future Biographers or Commentators on the Biography of Robert Louis Stevenson.
14. Ibid. *Dead Man's Chest*.

CHAPTER XIII

1. *Recollections of Robert Louis Stevenson in the Pacific* by Arthur Johnstone.
2. Ibid. *Letters of R.L. Stevenson*, Vil. III, p. 65.
3. The title of the original English edition of 1846 was 'Narrative of a four months residence among the natives of a valley of the Marquesas Islands'.

188

4.   Ibid. *Letters of R.L. Stevenson*, Vol. III, p. 66.
5.   See *Island Nights Entertainments*, introduction by Lisa St. Aubin de Teran (published 1987), p. 127.
6.   Gauguin died in the Marquesas Islands in 1903.
7.   Ibid. *Dead Man's Chest*, Nicholas Rankin, p. 260.
8.   Ibid. *Letters of R.L. Stevenson*, Vol. III, p. 120.
9.   Published in *Songs of Travel*.

CHAPTER XIV

1.   *In the South Seas*, Part IV, 'The Gilberts', p. 275.
2.   Ibid. *Letters of R.L. Stevenson*, Vol. III, p. 131.
3.   Ibid. *Letters of Robert Louis Stevenson*, Vol. III, pp. 124 & 125.
4.   Ibid. *Dead Man's Chest*.
5.   Ibid. *Letters of Robert Louis Stevenson*, Vol. III, p. 129.
6.   Ibid. *In the South Seas*, p. 2.
7.   Ibid. *In the South Seas*, p. 275.
8.   Prefatory note by Mrs. R.L. Stevenson to *The Wrecker*.
9.   Ibid. *Songs of Travel* XXV.
10. Ibid. *The Wrecker* by Robert Louis Stevenson, Heinemann, pp. 189-190.
11. Ibid. *Robert Louis Stevenson*, Pope Hennessy.
12. Ibid. *Voyage to Windward*, Furnas.
13. Ibid. *Voyage to Windward*, p. 310.
14. Ibid. *Letters of R.L. Stevenson*, Vol. III, pp. 150 & 151.
15. Stevenson to James, August 1890.
16. *Rudyard Kipling: His Life and Work* by Charles Carrington, 1955.
17. Ibid. *Rudyard Kipling*, H. James to E. Gosse, 6th August 1891.
18. Ibid. *Life and Letters of Sir Edmund Gosse* by The Hon. Evan Charteris.
19. Ibid. National Library of Edinburgh, *Voyage to Windward*.

CHAPTER XV

1.   *Letters of Henry Adams 1858-91* edited by Worthington Chauncey Ford, 1930.
2.   Ibid. *Letters of Henry Adams*.
3.   A good biography of Henry Adams is by Elizabeth Stevenson.
4.   *Our Samoan Adventure* by Fanny and R.L. Stevenson, pp. 54-55.
5.   Being correspondence addressed by R.L.S. to Sidney Colvin, Vol. IV, November 1890-October 1894.
6.   Ibid. *Our Samoan Adventure*.
7.   *This Life I've Loved* by Isobel Field. Belle's second husband was Salisbury Field, playwright and protégé of her mother's.
8.   Ibid. *This Life I've Loved*, p. 264.
9.   Ibid. *Voyage to Windward*, p. 453, n. 27.
10. First printed in Samoa, then in *Island Nights Entertainments*.
11. Ibid. *Robert Louis Stevenson*, Pope Hennessy.

CHAPTER XVI

1. First published in 1892, having appeared serially under the title of *Uma* in *Illustrated London News*.
2. Page 242.
3. Ibid. *Our Samoan Adventure*.
4. Ibid. *Our Samoan Adventure*, p. 55.
5. See *Vailima Letters* to Sidney Colvin.
6. Lady Jersey wrote an account of it in *Nineteenth Century*, January 1893.
7. Ibid. *R.L.S.: A Life Study*, p. 304.
8. *Memories of Vailima* by Isobel Strong and Lloyd Osbourne, 1903.
9. *St. Ives: The Adventures of a French Prisoner of War in England*, Richard Drew Publishing, Edinburgh, p. 47.
10. Ibid. *Vailima Letters*. Being correspondence addressed by Robert Louis Stevenson to Colvin.
11. Ibid. *Vailima Letters*, p. 287.
12. Ibid. *Memories of Vailima*.
13. John Connell.
14. Ibid. *The Letters of Robert Louis Stevenson*, Vol. IV, 1892-1894.
15. *Pall Mall Magazine*, December 1901.
16. *Stevenson's Home Life at Vailima* by Lloyd Osbourne.
17. Ibid. *Voyage to Windward*, p. 342.
18. Ibid. *Letters of Robert Louis Stevenson*, Vol. IV, p. 10.

CHAPTER XVII

1. Published in *Horizon*, January-June 1946, now in book form.
2. Some portraits by Raeburn in *Virginibus Puerisque* - a series of essays.
3. Henley's letter to Colvin, November 10th, 1892.
4. *Collected Poems*, pp. 183-184.
5. Ibid. *The Life of Robert Louis Stevenson*, Rosaline Masson.
6. Ibid. *Letters of Robert Louis Stevenson*, Vol. IV, p. 306.
7. Ibid. *Horizon*. Novelist-Philosophers, January-June 1946, p. 307.
8. Ibid. *Memories of Vailima*.
9. Appendix, *Vailima Letters*, p. 361.
10. *Weir of Hermiston*, p. 114.
11. Ibid. James Pope Hennessy.

EPILOGUE

1. Ashley Mss.5087.23 British Library.
2. Ibid. Sanchez.
3. Muir, *Robert Louis Stevenson*, Modern Scott, Autumn 1931, p. 201.

Bibliography

Acland, Alice, *Caroline Norton* (1948).

Bacon's Essays, Golden Treasury series (1939).

Balfour, Graham, *The Life of Robert Louis Stevenson*, 2 vols. (1901).

Boodle, Adele, *R.L.S. and his Sine Qua Non* (1929).

Buckley, J.H., *William Ernest Henley : A Study in the Counter-Decadence of the 'Nineties* (1945).

Calder, Jenni, *R.L.S. : A Life Study* (1980).

Charteris, The Hon. Evan, *The Life and Letters of Sir Edmund Gosse* (1931).

Colvin, Sidney (ed.), *The Letters of Robert Louis Stevenson* (vol. I).

Connell, John, *W.E. Henley* (1949).

Daiches, David, *Robert Louis Stevenson and His World* (1973).

Elwin, Malcolm, *The Strange Case of Robert Louis Stevenson* (1950).

Ferguson, De Lancey, *Robert Louis Stevenson's Letters to Charles Baxter* (1956).

Ford, Worthington Chauncey (ed.), *Letters to Henry Adams (1858-1891)*, (1930).

Furnas, J.C., *Voyage to Windward* (1952).

Gray, Robert Q., *The Labour Aristocracy in Victorian Edinburgh* (1976).

Hayter, Alethea, *Opium and the Romantic Imagination* (1968).

Henley, W.E., R.A.M.S., *Pall Mall Magazine* (1901).

Horizon, 'Novelist-Philosophers' (January-June 1946).

Kinghorn, Alexander Manson and Alexander Law (ed.), *Poems by Allan Ramsay and Robert Fergusson* (1974).

Lang, Andrew, *Adventures among Books* (1905).

Low, Will, *A Chronicle of Friendships (1873-1900)* (1908).

Lucas, E.V., *The Colvins and their Friends* (1928).

Mackay, Margaret, *The Violent Friend* (1968).

Masson, Rosaline, *The Life of Robert Louis Stevenson* (1923).

Miller, Karl, *Cockburn's Millennium* (1975.

Muir, E., *Robert Louis Stevenson, Modern Scot* (1931).

Pope Hennessy, James, *Robert Louis Stevenson* (1974).

Rankin, Nicholas, *Dead Man's Chest : Travels after Robert Louis Stevenson* (1986).

191

Sanchez, Nellie van de Grift, *The Life of Mrs. Robert Louis Stevenson* (1920).

Smith, Janet Adam (ed.) *Collected Poems by Robert Louis Stevenson* (1971).

Smith, Janet Adam, *Henry James and Robert Louis Stevenson* (1948).

Steuart, J.A., *Robert Louis Stevenson, Man and Writer* (1924).

Stevenson, Elizabeth, *Henry Adams : a biography* (1955).

Stevenson, Margaret, 'Diary' (1855).

Stevenson, Robert Louis, *Prayers written at Vailima* (1908).

Strong, Isobel, *This Life I've Loved* (1937).

Strong, Isobel and Lloyd Osbourne, *Memories of Vailima* (1903).

Swinnerton, Frank, *R.L. Stevenson : A Critical Study* (1924).

Vailima Letters being correspondence addressed by Robert Louis Stevenson to Sidney Colvin (Nov. 1890-Oct. 1894), (1895).

Manuscript material. National Library of Scotland, MSS 4383, MSS 90, MSS 8790.

Manuscript material. British Library. Ashley 5087.

Index

197